The Global Scramble for the Nomads' Backyard

A History and a Remedy

Mohamed Mohamud Abdi

CLEAR PRESS

Birmingham – UK

Published by Clear Press, an imprint of Safis Publishing Limited, Birmingham, UK.
www.clear-press.net

ISBN   978-1-906342-47-0 (paperback)
        978-1-906342-48-7 (ebook)

First Edition

Version Identifier: 22111701

Contents

Contents 3

Introduction 5

The History of the Scramble 7

The Consequences of the Scramble for the Somali Region 25

The Impacts of the Scramble Beyond the Somali Region 59

The Remedy 83

Lessons from Other Countries 105

Epilogue 127

Notes and Bibliography 135

Index 139

Introduction

One day, a group of nomads gathered under a tree somewhere in the Ogaden Basin for their daily routine assembly, which began with tuning into the news on a radio. The main topic of the news that day was the cold war between the Eastern bloc led by the USSR and the US-led NATO alliance. After they listened to the news, an elderly man asked the group whether they knew what the two alliances were fighting over, and they replied that they did not understand the reason behind their conflict.

The elderly man raised his voice, apparently to show his dissatisfaction with their answer, and said 'They are fighting over your backyard. All of them want to take it over and the place is too small to be divided and shared by so many countries.' Although the nomads had no idea about the level of prosperity in the first and the second world, they knew they were industrialised nations and therefore were surprised by the elderly man's assertion that these advanced nations were after their little pastureland. But after a lengthy talk in which the elderly gentleman informed them of what he had witnessed in their backyard and explained in detail what the foreign oil companies are looking for in their backyard, they were convinced of the dangers the superpowers and their alliances posed to them and their land.

In this book, the nomads are the inhabitants of the Somali Region and the nomads' backyard is the oil-rich Ogaden Basin. The scramble for the geological resources in the Ogaden Basin, the consequent menace and how to repair the damage resulting from the scramble are the main topics of the book.

The quest for fossil fuels in the Ogaden Basin was the main reason behind the foreign powers' intrusion into that piece of land, and in their pursuit of the region's natural energy resources, they fought over the control of the Basin. Some of them occupied it for that goal, and others allied themselves with the occupant to get their share of the sought-after fortune. The scramble started in 1915, intensified after the Second World War, and continues to the present day. The different stages of the scramble as well as its impacts on the region and beyond will be reviewed. Specifically, its effects on the living conditions of the inhabitants, the environment and the natural resources, on peace and stability in the Somali Region, the Horn and the wider world will be examined. The first chapter of the book deals with the history of the global scramble for oil and gas in the Ogaden Basin. The second and third chapters are about the consequences of the scramble for the inhabitants of the Somali Region, the Horn of Africa and global peace.

The historical overview will be followed by recommended remedies for the scramble madness, which will be outlined in chapter four. Economic, social, security and human rights considerations are the basis for the remedy. The aims of the remedy are to give immediate relief to the victims of the scramble madness, repair the damage to the environment and the economy and introduce a long-term management framework for the geological resources.

In chapter five, experiences from other countries will be presented. The lessons from other countries consist of two different models, namely the Norwegian and Nigerian experiments. In terms of success, the experiments of the two countries are contrasting; however, both have useful elements that can be learned from.

The last chapter of the book (chapter six) will cover the ongoing discussion of the nomads regarding the future of their natural energy resources. The ongoing debate under the tree is a retrospective reflection of the scramble, an assessment of the current situation of the oil and gas project and the future plans for the protection and optimal utilisation of the geological resources.

1

The History of the Scramble

Following the industrial revolution, fossil fuels became the dominant energy source in the 19th century, and the use of oil by the electricity and transportation industries increased the demand for fossil fuels and set the stage for the rapid growth of the oil industry. In response to the growing demand for oil, many new oil companies were formed at the beginning of the 20th century, and existing ones were enlarged. Oil companies were established in the industrialised countries of Europe and North America, but as the demand for oil skyrocketed, they quickly moved to other parts of the world in search of oil reserves. The Ogaden region was one of the places where the search for oil began at the beginning of the 20th century, and petroleum seeps that were found in the region in the 19th century became the seeds of the scramble for its natural resources.

The quest for the geological resources of the Somali Regional State (Ogaden, or the Somali Region) by foreigners began before the annexation of the region by Ethiopia. The first actual exploratory surveys were conducted by an American company called Standard Oil Company. The company was given exploration concessions by Ethiopia in 1915 and, in the same year, it began preliminary explorations surveys in the Ogaden region, which were concluded in 1920. The exploration work took place under the guidance of the occupying forces in limited areas before the completion of the first Ethiopian occupation of the Somali Region. Those limited surveys showed positive results, which encouraged further searches for natural energy resources. However, the oil exploration operations were terminated due to related issues: the Italian occupation of Ethiopia, the Second World War, the British takeover of Italian-occupied territories in the Horn and the subsequent British military administration of Ethiopia and most of the Somali land.

Exploration of the Ogaden geological resources resumed in earnest after the Second World War, following an understanding between the American President Franklin D. Roosevelt and the Ethiopian emperor Haile Selassie. The two men met in Cairo, Egypt in 1945, and at that meeting, the Ethiopian Emperor requested American help for the reoccupation of the Ogaden, which was at the time under British administration. He used the Somali Region's natural resources as a bargaining chip when persuading the US government to help him with the reoccupation of the region. He promised the US government that he would give American oil companies exploration rights over the geological resources of the Somali Region in exchange for the US's backing of Ethiopia's reoccupation efforts. At the time, the British government was administering both Ethiopia and all Somali territories except Djibouti and was planning to reunite the four Somali territories under its administration. The British plan, which Haile Selassie lobbied against, failed because of the opposition of the other big powers (Russia, France, the US and Italy) to it.

Following the deal between the Ethiopian emperor and the US president, the US government helped Ethiopia to reoccupy the Ogaden by rejecting the British proposal for the Somali territories' reunification and by supporting and recognizing Ethiopia's claims over the Ogaden. The American backing was crucial to Ethiopia's reoccupation of the Ogaden and in recognition of that important support, Haile Selassie promptly fulfilled the promise he made in the Cairo meeting to Franklin D. Roosevelt and gave the US companies exploration concession rights in the Ogaden before the reoccupation of the region.

American and other Western oil companies began large-scale fossil fuel explorations in the region in the 1940s and 1950s. A US oil company, Sinclair Oil Corporation, took the lead and was later joined by other US companies, such as Tenneco Oil Exploration. The American companies started their exploration operations in the 1940s and although their activities were hampered by the ongoing conflict between the indigenous inhabitants and the Ethiopian occupants, they sporadically continued their work officially until 1974, when they left the country because of the regime change there.

Sinclair Oil Corporation came to the region in 1945 but because of anti-scramble demonstrations from the locals, the British administrators cancelled the company's first exploration attempt in the Wardheer area. Gewerkschaft Elwerath, a German oil company, carried out exploration surveys in the Wardheer area in the period 1959-67. Sinclair resumed work after the British rendered up most of the Ogaden region to Ethiopia in 1948 and by the end of 1960, Tenneco Oil Exploration, another American company, joined the scramble. Tenneco discovered the Calub and Hilala gas fields in 1972 and estimated the extent of the gas reserves of the two places in 1973 and 1974, respectively. The company also discovered a non-commercial oil reserve in Hilala in 1973. Although Tenneco confirmed the existence of a huge commercially viable amount of gas reserves in Calub and Hilala, it was not able to extract the gas because of the strong opposition to the exploration activities by the inhabitants and the consequent war between the occupants and the indigenous resistance.

Despite the discoveries, the exploration activities of the Western companies were paralysed by the conflict, and the oil companies left without accomplishing anything. They did not get any return for their investment, and the exploration wells they drilled and the general exploration surveys they conducted were taken over by the Soviet Petroleum Exploration Expedition (SPEE) after Ethiopia joined the socialist alliance and terminated its friendship treaty with the USA. The change in the alliance was the result of a regime change in Ethiopia in 1974 and the 1977-78 Ogaden war, in which the Communist alliance led by the Soviet Union supported Ethiopia. The Soviet company expanded exploration activities and further developed the gas fields in the 1980s.

For the inhabitants of the region, the illegal exploration activities were largely harmful and had adverse effects on the peace of the region and the livelihoods of the indigenous population. Some earthen roads in the exploration areas, which Gewerkschaft Elwerath built for exploration purposes but were used by the public

9

afterwards, were the only beneficial mark they left in the region.

The SPEE began exploration work during the 1980s and continued its operations there until the regime change in 1991 in which the Ethiopian Derg government led by Mengistu Haile Mariam was ousted and replaced by the EPRDF government led by Meles Zenawi. The Soviet Union was given exploration rights over the Ogaden natural resources as a reward for its support for Ethiopia's reoccupation efforts in the Ogaden after the Somali people liberated over 90 percent of their land during the 1977-78 Ogaden war. The SPEE made huge discoveries of gas reserves in the Ogaden Basin and drilled a large number of gas wells, some of which were ready for production before the SPEE's operations ended. The SPEE made further discoveries of extensive gas reserves in Calub and Hilala in the 1980s, which were estimated at the time at 118 billion cubic meters. The Soviet oil company ceased the exploration activities after the toppling of the Derg regime in 1991 and left the country afterwards because of the overthrow of the government that gave it the exploration concession.

In the period 1950-1991, between 40 and 50 wells were drilled. The two images below show 31 of those wells. Sinclair Oil Corporation drilled 17 of the wells, Tenneco Oil Exploration drilled 8 wells, the SPEE drilled 16, and Oil Hunt Company and Gewerkschaft Elwerath each drilled 1 well. The companies that drilled the first 43 wells belong to the USA, Russia and Germany, and the three countries' respective shares are 26, 16, and 1.

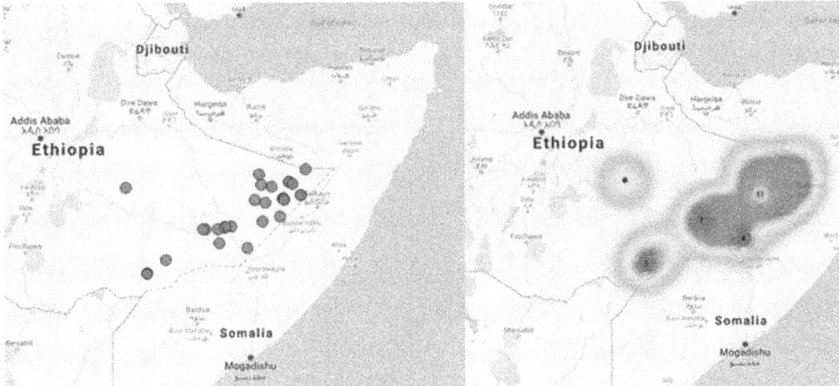

Image 1.1: Locations of drilled wells

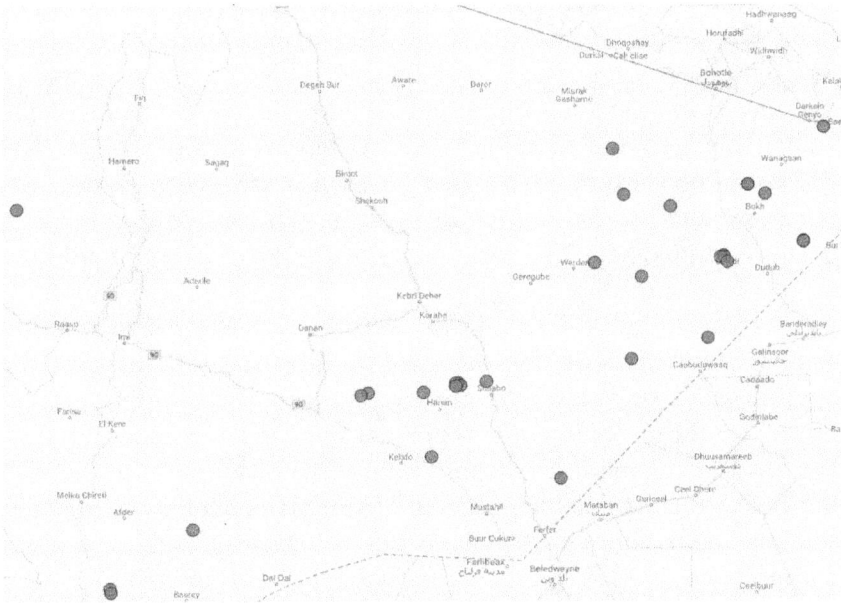

Image 1.2: Locations of drilled wells

Many more wells were drilled after that period by companies from different countries and continents, and in total over 60 wells are drilled. However, most of the recent drillings were done by Chinese companies, Zhongyuan Petroleum Exploration Bureau (ZPEB), Petro Trans Company Ltd and POLY-GCL. The latter held the main contract and led the development operations of the natural gas and crude oil extraction in the Ogaden Basin until recently.

The Ethiopian People's Revolutionary Democratic Front (EPRDF) regime, which came to power in 1991, first tried to run the gas and oil project through a government-owned company, the Kalub Gas Share Company. In 1994, the government requested international financial agencies and Western governments to finance the project, the cost of which was estimated at $130.8 million at the time. The World Bank's International Development Association (IDA) pledged in 1994 to give a loan of $74.3 million, on the condition that the government privatised the Kalub Gas Share Company. The African Development Bank agreed to contribute $27 million, and the government of the Netherlands promised to invest $4 million. Although the World Bank disbursed some portions of the agreed loan at the initial stage, it stopped the payment of the loan it pledged and afterwards pulled out from the project. The Ethiopian government negated the promise to privatise the company, and for that reason the bank suspended releasing the loan that it had pledged. The withdrawal of the World Bank made the project unsustainable.

To salvage the crumbling project, the Ethiopian Privatisation Agency invited four international companies to bid for the government's stake in the company. The aim of the bid was to get buyers for the government's 95 percent share in the company, which the World Bank made a precondition for the resumption of the loan but failed to get a sellable price. The Ethiopian government claimed that the companies' offers were not satisfactory and as a result withdrew the bid for the sale of its stake in the company.

Although it rejected selling its shares in the company, it continued the search for foreign investors. In subsequent bids, the government signed memoranda of understanding with some companies but again failed to sell its 95 percent share in the company, as demanded by the World Bank. The government claimed to have spent an estimated amount of $97 million on the first phase of the Calub project and wanted to recover that money through the sale of its shares. The oil companies were not ready to pay that amount, and the bank made it clear that it would not resume the payment of the loan before the full privatisation of the Kalub Gas Share Company.

Despite the failure to secure investment and the pulling out of the World Bank, it continued the share-selling game, which it conducted from the outset and for some time, mainly to raise money for the project. However, after repeated attempts by the government to sell its 95 percent share to private companies, it again failed to convince foreign oil companies to buy shares in the Kalub Gas share Company at the price it offered. Additionally, the security situation further discouraged oil companies from making a long-term commitment, and as result, the gas and oil project in the Ogaden Basin reached a dead end.

After the Ethiopian government realised the failure of its first strategy, it did not change its goal but came up with a different tactic of securing investment, by introducing concession bids for the gas fields. Instead of selling its shares in the Kalub Gas Share Company, it began to sell the gas fields.

Following the collapse of the deal between the Ethiopian government and the World Bank, it became clear to the government that it would not be able to get external funding and at the same time own and run the gas business. Additionally, Ethiopia is very keen to exploit the Ogaden gas but does not have the expertise or the funding for the exploration and extraction of oil and gas, and for that reason the country can never realise that goal without external support. The failure of the first strategy necessitated a rethink, which led to a change of approach toward the project. The government decided to give concessions to private companies that have the technological and financial capacity to carry out the project.

Since 1999, the EPRDF regime has given exploration rights to many companies from different continents, including Methanol from Russia, Petronas from Malaysia, GAIL India Limited from India, Si-Tech International Limited (SIL) from Jordan, Southwest Energy (HK) Ltd. and Petro Trans Company Ltd from Hong Kong, Lundin East Africa from Sweden, Sicor Inc. from the USA, Africa

Oil from Canada, New Age (African Global Energy) Ltd. from the UK and Zhongyuan Petroleum Exploration Bureau (ZPEB) from China. POLY-GCL Petroleum Group Holdings Limited is a Chinese company that used to hold the main contract of oil and gas exploration rights until 21 September 2022.

Nearly all the companies that were given exploration concessions by the EPRDF regime during its 27-year rule of Ethiopia left the region before the end of their contract period, and some of them prior to the commencement of their exploration work. Security concerns and disagreements with the government were the main reasons given for the termination of the contracts.

The Ethiopian government contacted and signed contracts with potential partners to get the funding and the technology required to reactivate the stalled project. In the long term, the government also expected to gain technology through partnerships with foreign companies. Many companies signed memoranda of understanding or agreements with the government, but nearly all of them pulled out from the project in the end. For brevity reasons, we will mention as examples only a few of the companies that made deals with the government.

In December 1999, Ethiopia announced that it had signed a $1.4 billion joint venture deal with a US firm, Sicor Inc., to develop the Calub and Hilala gas fields and build a pipeline and processing units. The two sides agreed to form a joint venture, namely Gasoil Ethiopia Project (GEP), which the government owned 20 percent of and the rest was owned by Sicor Inc., to carry out the development of the gas fields. GEP planned to construct a 375-mile pipeline to transmit the gas to the town of Awash in the Afar region, on the country's main railway line and highway that connects it with Djibouti. A gas treatment plant and a refinery were to be constructed in Awash. The plant and a refinery would convert the gas and liquids into commercial fuels using gas to liquid (GTL) technology. The joint venture was expected to be operational within a year, with production slated to start in 2002. The agreement did not materialise, and the company withdrew from the project before the time scheduled for the commencement of the operation.

Following the departure of Sicor, the government reached a memorandum of understanding with Methanol, a Russian oil company, in 2002. The company agreed to invest $80-100 million in the initial stage to get in return a 50 percent share of the Calub gas fields. According to the development plan, the two parties agreed to construct four refinery and petroleum extraction plants within the Calub area. However, the plan was scrapped due to a lack of funding. The government claimed that the Russian company failed to fulfil the investment funding promise it made and as a result, the planned project did not kick off.

After the termination of the Methanol deal, the Ethiopian government awarded Si-Tech International Limited (SIL) in 2003 a license granting the company the right to develop the natural gas reserves in the Calub and Hilala localities in the Ogaden Basin. The company announced that it had allocated an initial capital investment of $1.5 billion for the development of the gas project. SIL had a plan to build a gas refinery plant, the construction of which was supposed to start in 2004. Additionally, the company intended to build an electric power station as well as fertiliser and cement factories. However, before the commencement of the work, the government revoked SIL's licence due to work postponement. The company admitted their failure to launch the project according to schedule and claimed that poor road conditions to the gas fields and the inflated price of steel prevented the work from starting on schedule. The government rejected the reasons given by the company and cancelled the contract in January 2006.

The Malaysian company Petronas became the chief contractor operating in the Ogaden Basin after it won a tender for the exploration and development of the Hilala and Calub gas fields in 2006. The company paid $80 million for the deal and, in addition to that, agreed to pay the Ethiopian government 3 percent royalty and 35 percent income tax. Ethiopia would also get a 5 percent share from the annual gas production. The company started work in 2007 and it carried out the drilling work through its Chinese subcontractor, ZPEB. The Obale facility of ZPEB was stormed by ONLF commandos in 2007, and that halted the exploration project.

Due to the fallout from the Obale attack and disagreements it had with the government, Petronas sold its shares to Southwest, a local company, and quit the project in 2010.

Following the pull out of Petronas, the government invited 7 companies to bid for the development of the Hilala and Calub gas fields and the exploration of 8 other blocks in the Ogaden Basin. Petro Trans, a Hong Kong-based Chinese company, was declared the winner and replaced Petronas. According to the deal, Petro Trans agreed to an upfront payment of $130 million to the Ethiopian government, and would also pay 35 percent income tax, 5 percent royalty as well as 5 percent from the annual production income to Ethiopia. The company also made an investment commitment of $4 billion for the development of the project. Despite the huge sums the company agreed to pay and invest, the agreement was cancelled by the government. In 2012, the Ethiopian government terminated the contract agreement it had with Petro Trans, accusing the company of failing to carry out operations on schedule.

In another part of the Ogaden Basin, namely El-Kuraan in Afdheer Zone, where blocks 7 and 8 are located, three companies signed a cooperation agreement and got a concession from the government to prospect for oil and gas there. The three companies, New Age (African Global Energy) Ltd from the UK, Africa Oil from Canada and East Exploration Limited from the UAE, confirmed the gas and oil discovered by Tenneco there in the 1970s. Although significant amounts of oil and gas were found in the two blocks, African oil and East Exploration Limited, which each owned a 30 percent stake in the blocks, withdrew from the project in 2014 and 2016, respectively. The British company, New Age Ltd, whose involvement in the project began in 2008 with a 15 percent share, gradually increased its stake in the project and became the sole operator in El-Kuraan reserves after taking over the shares of Africa Oil and East Exploration Limited. New Age Ltd conducted exploration surveys and made three discoveries of gas and oil in El-Kuraan; however, the amounts of oil and gas there are yet to be determined. The British company is also involved in the exploration of the Adigala Basin, which is in the Siti Zone in the northern part of the Somali Region.

Ethiopia made exploration and extraction contracts with many companies from various parts of the world in the period 1999-2011, but nearly all of those contracts were cancelled shortly after the signing of the agreements for security reasons or because of disagreement between the governments and the companies involved. The companies withdrew mainly after they realised the opposition to the project from the local people, which was expressed both in political and military terms. In other words, they pulled out because Ethiopia was not able to provide a safe environment for those companies in which they could conduct their business, and they felt misled by the government about the security situation. As a result of the armed conflict in the region and the resulting mistrust between the parties over the government's cover-up of the security risks, the scramble project lost direction and needed urgent rescue. Ethiopia neither has the technological know-how to extract gas and oil, nor the security capability to guard the wide area of the project, and therefore it sought external help to bridge both the technological and the security gaps.

Ethiopia saw China, the rising superpower as the right place to seek help. China has already undertaken a project of this type in a comparable situation, security wise. The neighbouring country of Sudan was in a civil war when the Chinese companies extracted the oil there and took part in the building of the pipelines that transport it from the south to the north.

The late Ethiopian Prime Minister, Meles Zenawi, paid a visit to China in 2011 and, during that visit, the Chinese government pledged to help Ethiopia with its economic programme in exchange for the takeover of the gas and oil exploration and extraction rights in the Somali Region. Following the agreement between the two countries, the Chinese government established a company to carry out the agreed oil and gas project. The POLY-GCL Petroleum and Natural Gas Investments Limited Ethiopian Branch, which is controlled and mainly financed by the government of China, was formed to help Ethiopia in the exploration, development and production of oil and natural gas in the Ogaden Basin.

POLY-GCL Petroleum Investment Limited is a joint venture of the Chinese government-owned China Poly Group Corporation and the Hong Kong-based Golden Concord Holdings Limited. The company has invested in the development and production of petroleum and natural gas extraction in the Ogaden Basin, and the project is financed by the China Development Bank, which is owned by the government of China.

POLY-GCL signed a contract agreement with the government of Ethiopia on 16 November 2013 to explore and develop a large area of the Ogaden Basin. According to the production sharing deal they signed, the company agreed to pay $100 million for the Calub and Hilala fields. The net production revenue ratio between Ethiopia and the company was set at 15:85. Although it would be able to gain further income through land rent, income tax, and royalties, Ethiopia would get only 15 percent of the annual production revenue.

POLY-GCL got a concession for 10 exploration and development blocks with a total area of 117,151 square kilometres and began its exploration activities in 2014. The company was aiming to develop the natural gas reserves in the gas fields of Hilala, Calub and Dohar and was also searching for more reserves in another large part of its license area. It had discovered large new reserves of natural gas in 2018 at Dohar, which is located between Hilala and Calub. Additionally, the company found more gas reserves in the exploration fields of Hilala and Calub. POLY-GCL subcontracted the collection of seismic data to another Chinese company, BGP Geo Services, in an area measuring approximately 93,000 square kilometres in the Ogaden Basin. The gas fields at Dohar are estimated to hold over 3 trillion cubic feet of gas. The total gas reserves of the Ogaden basin are estimated at about 7 trillion cubic feet (TCF) by the American company Netherland, Sewell & Associates Inc. (NSAI) in August 2022.

POLY-GCL drilled new exploration wells and conducted 3D and 2D seismic surveys on the new wells, as well as the ones drilled by the American and Russian companies, using new technology.

The modern technology enabled POLY-GCL to get different insights into the existing structure oil reserves in Hilala, which were first identified by Tenneco. In 2018, POLY-GCL confirmed that there was a large quantity of oil there. The company undertook successful exploration surveys and found oil in two wells in Hilala. First results indicated the prospect of commercial quantities of crude oil reserves; however, the exact amount of the oil is still unknown.

POLY-GCL and the governments of Ethiopia and Djibouti also decided in subsequent agreements to develop the gas fields. They signed a memorandum of understanding in February 2019 detailing how to transport the gas and develop the Ogaden Basin gas fields. According to the tripartite deal, POLY-GCL would construct a 700-900 km pipeline that would connect the existing gas fields in the Ogaden Basin to a Djibouti coastal town to transport the gas. The company would also build a gas treatment plant in Djibouti and the gas treatment plant would convert the gas into Liquefied Natural Gas (LNG). Further, the Chinese company planned to export the LNG to China with special LNG vessels.

Damerdjog, in the Arta region, is the town in Djibouti where the gas treatment plant was to be built. According to the plan of the recently cancelled contract, the LNG plant would occupy an area of approximately fifty hectares. The main processing and supplementary facilities of the plant included a feed gas pre-treatment unit, a liquefaction unit, LNG storage, a transmission system, and production and administration buildings.

The total cost of the development project (the pipeline, the liquefaction plant and an export terminal), which POLY-GCL and the governments of Ethiopia and Djibouti agreed, was estimated at $4 billion, and the project would be financed by POLY-GCL. According to the plan, the gas pipeline would transport 12 billion cubic metres of natural gas from Ethiopia to Djibouti every year and 10 million cubic metres of liquefied natural gas would be exported to China annually. Ethiopia expected to earn about $1.5 billion every year from the gas in the first stage and up to $7 billion in a few years' time, when the production reached full capacity.

The regime change in Ethiopia in 2018 did not affect the tripartite agreement. The new prime minister of Ethiopia was a member of the government that had made the deals with POLY-GCL and Djibouti regarding the Somali Regional State's natural resources, and his government approved the previous agreements regarding that issue.

The tripartite agreement outlined how to fund and carry out the project, as well as the parties' respective shares of the production revenue and other benefits. But the deal neither gave the primary owners of the gas a role in the running of the project, nor did it mention their portion of the revenue.

A few months after he came into power in 2018, the Ethiopian prime minister was asked about the sharing formula of the revenue from the natural gas in the Somali state. He replied in vague terms that the natural resources belonged to all Ethiopians irrespective of where they were found and added that the government's plan was to allocate 5–10 percent of the revenue from the natural resources for the development of the places where the natural resources were found. He said that this 5–10 percent allocation to the resource-producing places was customary in many African countries. His statement sparked outrage in the Somali Region and immediately instigated a campaign spearheaded by the regional administration to get clarification from the federal government on that burning issue. Whether it was in response to the Somali demand or not, the federal government passed a new law in the upper chamber of parliament in June 2019 stating for the first time how the federal government and regional states would share the income from natural resources. The law was supposed to be effective from 2013 in the Ethiopian calendar (2020–2021).

The new law on natural resource income sharing outlines how the revenue from the resources, which in this case consists of oil profit, taxes and royalties, should be distributed amongst the tiers of the government. The regional state where the resource is found gets 50 percent of the revenue, the federal government takes 25 percent, and the other regional states share the remaining 25 percent amongst themselves. Of the 25 percent that the federal government gets, it distributes to the regional states through a budgetary subsidy mechanism, and the region where the resource is found receives its share from that portion of the revenue. The law also assigns 10 percent of the 50 percent of the resource-producing region to the vicinity where the natural resource is extracted as compensation for the environmental and economic damage related to the extraction.

POLY-GCL was different from all the other companies because of the political, financial and military backing of the company by the three governments involved in the scramble (China, Ethiopia and Djibouti) since it got the contract. The shared interest of these three governments in the development of the gas project and the commitment they made in realizing that goal gave POLY-GCL an advantage over its competitors and enabled it to stay in the region for over 9 years. But it could not succeed in accomplishing what the other companies failed to deliver.

On 21 September 2022, the Ethiopian Ministry of Mines and Petroleum announced the termination of the POLY-GCL contract. Given Ethiopia's dire need for economic and political support and China's significant role in Ethiopia, in terms of political backing and economic development assistance, the timing of the termination was a surprise to many observers. China has been supporting the Ethiopian government's position in the Security Council over the Tigray conflict and has ongoing development projects and extensive trade with Ethiopia. However, despite the strong political backing for POLY-GCL from all involved governments, signs of practical failures were on the horizon long before the cancelation announcement.

Ethiopia's parliament approved the pipeline construction in December 2019 and the pipeline construction was supposed to start in the same year, but the work of the pipeline never started. The ongoing civil war, which affected the planned pipeline route, seemingly made the original plan unfeasible. The LNG was to be exported from 2021 according to the plan, but nothing was done in that regard, and even the commencement date of the construction of the treatment plant in Djibouti was not announced. The gas development project was already several years behind schedule when the contract was cancelled. Besides that, disagreements between Ethiopia and POLY- GCL over financial commitments, which recently emerged, also indicated the possibility of the termination of the contract.

The Ethiopian government accused the Chinese company of failing to register 30 percent of its $4.2 billion total investment at the National Bank of Ethiopia as required, and of failing to pay an annual contribution for the development of host communities, which it claimed was stipulated in the contract. The government claimed that the contribution, amounting to $50,000 per year intended as compensation for locals in the Ogaden Basin, had not been paid since 2017 by the company, and the total outstanding amount is $1.7 million. The company was given an ultimatum in March 2022 to meet the demand, and the government warned that it would terminate the contract unless the company resolved the financial issues.

Since the locals are excluded from the scramble project, the so-called community contribution mentioned in the ultimatum letter and a small amount of oil tax money from the federal government to the regional government were surprise news in the region. The federal government did not talk to the locals about the community contribution from the oil companies, but it paid insignificant amounts, which it said was tax collected from oil companies and was intended for the development of the area affected by the project. At the end of 2021, the federal government paid 50 million Birr to the regional authorities, and in June 2022 the regional authorities received a cheque in the amount of 113 million Birr from the federal government. This tax payment was the first financial payment related to the project, and although it was a small step in the right direction, its effect was minimal on the locals' perception of the project because of their exclusion from it.

The financial and organisational inability of POLY-GCL to develop the gas project was the reason given by the Ethiopian government for the cancellation of the contract. The Ethiopian government added that it is looking for international oil companies to step in and fill the vacuum.

In addition to the aforementioned difficulties, the country is now in the midst of a civil war, with unpredictable consequences for the fate of the republic. Thus, the Ogaden gas and oil project is in practical terms on hold for the time being. However, despite the delay resulting from the civil war and the political, economic and logistical problems, Ethiopia's determination to carry out the project has not changed. As it did in the past, Ethiopia is once again putting the Ogaden Basin project out to tender, primarily to get immediate cash relief and to find a business partner that can reactivate the project.

2

The Consequences of the Scramble for the Somali Region

2.1 Endless Conflict

Since the invasion of the Ogaden region for the sake of the intertwined aims of the annexation of the region and the scramble for its natural resources began, there has been resistance to the occupation and the subsequent attempt to plunder the natural resources of the Somali people. Ethiopia and its partners in the scramble decided to crush the people and subjugate them in order to thereafter rob them of their natural resources, but the inhabitants could not accept being enslaved, nor would they condone the looting of their resources. Thus, a conflict between the occupants and the inhabitants of the region began with the first incursion of the conquering army into the region and continues unabated to this day, except for periodical respites for revitalisation.

The Ogaden conflict has been in the spotlight since the start of the occupation, and it drew global attention to the region during the 1977-78 Ogaden war due to the internationalisation of the conflict. Countries from four continents and from both the Eastern and Western alliances, including the superpowers, were involved in the 1977-78 Ogaden war, and as a result it attracted wide coverage from local and international media.

However, despite the huge coverage of the war and the internationalisation of the conflict, the root causes of the war and the inhabitants' perspective on the conflict did not get due attention. Because of the unequal resources of the conflicting parties, the interest-guided system of international relations and the inhabitants' lack of representation in international arenas, the indigenous people were not able to tell their side of the story to the world, and thus the occupant has had an easy ride in distorting the truth.

In the two-part historical work entitled 'A history of the Ogaden (Western Somali) Struggle for Self-Determination', the conflict and its root causes are extensively covered, and the historical events detailed in chronological order from the perspective of the indigenous people of the Somali Region. Additionally, the effects of the conflict on human rights and the living conditions of the people are detailed there too.

The struggle for freedom was triggered by the occupation and the ensuing repression through which the occupant sought to maintain the annexation. The ongoing struggle for freedom since the annexation of the region by Ethiopia, and the persistent repression, led to enormous adverse effects on livelihoods and human rights in the region. In this book, we will briefly discuss the conflict and its consequences.

Abyssinia's dream of expanding its territory southwards and eastwards became apparent during the 14th century, when it invaded several Muslim emirates, including Ifat Hadiya, Dawaro, Sidama Bali and Adal. However, because of the resistance led by the Adal Sultanate, it did not realise that dream until the elimination of that Sultanate in the 19th century.

Following the European scramble for Africa, which led to the partition of the continent, but that paradoxically strengthened the position of the Ethiopian state both militarily and politically, Ethiopia resumed its territorial expansion efforts. The European powers who came to Africa to divide it amongst themselves not only spared the Ethiopian state from the scramble, but also gave it a share in the land grab and assisted it in conquering the lands designated for it.

After the death of Emperor Johannes IV on 10 March 1889 at the battle of Matemma (against the Mahdist forces), Menelik II acceded to the Ethiopian throne and assumed the title of King of Kings. After having consolidated his rule all over the country, Menelik turned his attention to the issue of land expansion, an issue he already acted upon before his coronation as king of Ethiopia.

The Abyssinian land expansion efforts resumed in earnest when Menelik became King of Shoa in 1878. During his rule of Shoa, he concentrated on his southward expansion and was successful in that endeavour. After he acquired a large amount of arms and political support from the main European powers operating in the Horn of Africa (France, Italy and Britain), he conquered huge areas southwest and southeast of Shoa. Within ten years, he more than tripled Shoan and thereby Ethiopian territory in the south, and the territories he annexed in that period included Gurage, Kestane and Arsi.

After these conquests, Menelik planned for the elimination of the sultanate of Harar, a city state that inherited the Somali Adal Sultanate, which had defended the Somali Region from the Abyssinian aggression since the 14th century. Following the British occupation of Egypt in 1882, Britain took over the Egyptian administrations in the Horn, which included Harar and northern coastal Somali towns. In 1884, Britain ordered the Egyptian army to leave the city and threatened to stop wage payments to any official who disobeyed, a move that appeared to be paving the way for the Abyssinian invasion of Harar. The removal of the Egyptian forces was completed in 1885.

'Amir Abdalla Mohammed was reinstalled as governor of the city after the Egyptian withdrawal but after the Amir took over the reign, Britain suddenly demanded that he return 18 rifles it claimed were stolen from. Britain wanted to secure the borders of the Christian empire from the Muslims and the evacuation of the Egyptian army and the claim regarding the weapons were both part of the plot. On 27 March 1886, an Italian commercial and scientific expedition under Count Porro started from Zeila for Harar, and he was ambushed and killed at Arto, near Harar, and both the British and the Italians blamed the Amir of Harar for the massacre. On the pretext of that massacre, the Italians not only encouraged Menelik but also took part in the Abyssinian invasion of Harar, both militarily and politically'.[1]

Menelik invaded Harar only after he secured the backing of both Britain and Italy in 1886. In January 1887, a joint Italo-Abyssinian force descended on the city-state. The sultanate anticipated his invasion and strongly resisted, but it was not enough to defend against the invading alliance led by Menelik. With the political backing of Britain and direct Italian military support, Menelik conquered Harar on 6 January 1887. The recorded correspondence between Menelik and the British Consul in Aden shows that Britain was not only happy about the takeover but that they also tolerated the ensuing atrocities committed by the Abyssinians against the inhabitants of Harar and the surrounding areas. Harar was Menelik's final great conquest as king of Shoa, but as emperor since 1889, he continued his southward and eastward expansion further into the Ogaden and elsewhere.

In his capacity as king of Ethiopia, Menelik accelerated the land expansion campaign and vigorously fought on both diplomatic and military fronts to achieve his territorial goal. Emboldened by the military and political backing of the European imperialists, he wrote in 1891 his famous circular in which he demanded to be given a share of the partitioned Horn region and presented the future borders of his dream empire.

The Somali Region was one of the places Menelik had in mind when he was writing the circular to the major European powers, and the positive response to his circular and subsequent military support he got from these powers enabled him to conquer the Somali Region. Although the Ethiopian occupation of the Somali Region was prompted mainly by the hunt for its geological resources, the livestock resources of the region were another attraction of the invading army during the first stage of the conquest. The great famine of 1888–1892 and the wars of the 1890s devastated the subsistence Ethiopian economy. The huge and hungry Ethiopian army was pressing hard upon the resources of Abyssinia, and

---

[1] M M Abdi, *A history of the Ogaden (Western Somali) Struggle for Self Determination*, Part I (1300-2007), page 26.

because of this pressure, the occupation was accelerated and extended further to feed its hungry soldiers.

In the first phase of his occupation of the Somali Region, Menelik sent his troops from his base in Harar to the neighbouring Somali territories to terrorise the inhabitants and loot their livestock. The army undertook frequent raids into the region, killing the inhabitants indiscriminately, and then returned to their base with the looted livestock. Afterward, the Abyssinian Kingdom systematically extended its terror and looting to the whole region. Because of the limited resources in the Somali Region and the fact that the conquering army had to live off the backs of the conquered, the brutal Ethiopian occupation became more burdensome and traumatic to the indigenous inhabitants.

The search for oil worldwide and oil seeps found in the region drew the attention of oil companies. The petroleum companies decided to search for the presence of oil deposits in the Somali Region with the help of Ethiopia, and that development was the seed of the formation of the alliance for the scramble for the natural energy resources of the Ogaden. The oil companies that came for the exploitation of the geological resources of the Somali Region tried to gain access to the region's natural energy resources through the occupation forces and from there, an alliance made up of foreign oil companies and the occupant was established to conquer the Ogaden region, subjugate its inhabitants and then loot their natural resources.

The oil companies made agreements with Ethiopia before it completed the occupation of the region and since then, the partnership between the foreign oil companies and successive Ethiopian governments continued in its attempts to exploit the Somali Region's geological resources, though because of regime changes and conflict, concession contracts frequently changed hands among the involved oil companies.

Despite the change in the companies, the strategy and the practical tools of the scramble did not change. Since the Standard Oil Company made the first agreement with Ethiopia in 1915, the scramble approach was the same: to wreak havoc on the indigenous

29

people and the environment before robbing their resources. The militaristic means that the alliance for the scramble for the Ogaden's resources opted for at the start to achieve its looting goal remains unchanged.

The brutal invasion and looting of the region's resources triggered a response. The Somali people rejected the occupation, and a resistance, first led by the Dervishes, conducted the first organised armed operations against the occupants. Other successive resistance movements, some of which operate in the region to the present day, followed in the footsteps of the Dervishes. The persistent armed resistance has so far prevented the alliance for the scramble for the Ogaden's natural resources from achieving its aim.

In 1990 Dervish forces attacked Jigjiga. Sayyid Mohamed, the leader of the Dervishes, offered his assistance to the Somali people, who had recently suffered crippling livestock losses at the hands of the Ethiopians. In March 1900, a Dervish force of about 6,000 stormed the Ethiopian garrison at the wells of Jigjiga, and the Dervish army recovered much of the looted livestock in that action.

The oil companies halted their operations in the 1920s and left the region due mainly to the struggle for the defence of the region and its resources undertaken by the inhabitants, and because of the turmoil in the Horn that followed the Italian occupation of Ethiopia and the Ogaden in the 1930s, the Second World War, and the subsequent takeover of Italian administered territories in the Horn by Britain during the 1940s. The oil companies pulled out from the region and sought their fortunes elsewhere, notably in the Middle East, but they returned at the end of the Second World War. As mentioned earlier, their return was part of a deal reached between the US and Ethiopian leaders for the reoccupation of the region by Ethiopia. The Ogaden region was under British administration when, in 1945, Haile Selassie sought American help for the return of the Ogaden and in exchange promised to reward them with the exploitation of its resources. The deal materialised and the American companies reached the region before the British handover. However, the British administrator suspended their first exploration attempt because of demonstrations from the locals.

When Ethiopia eventually took over most of the region in 1948, the companies resumed their operations, but due to the strong resistance to the occupation and the scramble for the region's natural resources, the exploration work was conducted sporadically. Throughout the 1950s and 1960s, there were persistent uprisings spearheaded by the Somali Youth League (SYL) and the Nasrullah movements, but the resistance was not armed until 1963 when the resistance army that replaced the Dervishes was established.

Although unorganised, armed Somali resistance in the Ogaden clashed with Ethiopian troops six months after the independence of Somalia in 1960. The clashes were initially a response to the indiscriminate killing and afterwards were about tax collection, but they spread as nationalistic sentiment grew and Ethiopia decided to suppress the general uprising. After the completion of the reoccupation, the Nasrullah army, known as the Geysh, began in 1963 the first organised guerrilla war against the Ethiopian occupation forces in the region. In 1964, Ethiopia attacked Somalia for allegedly supporting the armed resistance in the Ogaden, and the two countries fought a brief war following that Ethiopian aggression.

The armed struggle led by Nasrullah ended due to a ceasefire between Ethiopia and Somalia and the subsequent détente policy pursued by Somalia, which sought to improve its relations with its neighbours and consequently reversed its support to the Somali resistance in the Horn region. The Western Somali Liberation Front (WSLF) inherited the struggle and took the leadership mantle during the 1970s and 1980s. The organisation led a successful liberation campaign in the 1970s: with the help of Somalia, it was able to liberate over 90 percent of the region in the period 1977-78. Unfortunately, that victory was reversed by a Soviet-led alliance from four continents that entered the war to forcibly reimpose the Ethiopian occupation of the Somali Region.

Al-Itihad and the Ogaden National Liberation Front (ONLF) replaced the WSLF at the beginning of the 1990s. Both organisations made strong armed resistance during the 1990s, though Al-Itihad left the battlefield by the end of that decade. In

2007, the ONLF conducted an operation on an exploration facility belonging to a Chinese oil company in Obale. That attack was the first direct attack on oil companies and was prompted by the ramping up of the exploration activities and the subsequent threat the intensification of the scramble posed to the environment and the geological resources of the region. The ONLF commanders claimed the action was necessitated by the threat the looting posed to the natural resources, which the inhabitants of the region felt, and which is undertaken by a foreign alliance united to take their natural riches from underneath their feet. The ONLF carried out the armed struggle until the Asmara peace deal in 2018.

The quest for the Somali Region's natural gas and oil reserves was one of the principal causes of the annexation of the region and the main reason for the continuation of the occupation, which in turn became the chief cause of all miseries in the Somali region. The natural bounty was supposed to bring prosperity to the indigenous people of the land in which it was found. However, so far, it has only been the source of suffering. In the following sections, we will examine the menace that originated from the scramble for the natural resources of the Somali Region.

2.2 Persistent Repression

After the occupation of Harar, Menelik began raids on the Somali Region, killing and torturing any one on sight and seizing their properties. The number of livestock seized by Menelik between 1890 and 1897 was estimated at 100,000 head of cattle, 200,000 head of camels, and 600,000 sheep and goats. Because the Abyssinians neither drink camel milk nor eat its meat, the seized camels were used principally as a bargaining asset with the owners, who were pressed to recover their looted camels with payment of cattle, sheep or goats.

Abyssinia was not only looting the properties of the indigenous people, but killing the people too in great numbers and in a cruel manner. Not only was the level of killing high, but the method of killing was even more shocking. As reported by independent observers and the British colonial authorities in the Horn region, the Abyssinian cruel killing included the cutting of women's breasts and skinning individuals while alive. The Somali victims were often from clans that had signed protection treaties with Britain and, at the time of the worst killing, Italy was claiming the whole of Ethiopia as its protectorate. Despite their promise of protection, these powers did not bother to condemn the atrocities, let alone intervene on behalf of the victims.

The Abyssinian atrocities of war crimes, crimes against humanity and genocide, as well as the property robbery that preceded the annexation, not only became perpetual, but their level rapidly increased and their scope widened. Because of the resistance to the occupation and the ensuing violation of human rights, the repression escalated and took different forms. Ethiopia wanted to maintain the annexation in the same forceful manner with which it conquered the region, and thus any attempt to undermine its grip on the region was harshly crushed. On the other hand, the determination to resist and the strength of the resistance were to some extent influenced by the level of brutality. In other words, the increased atrocities led to stronger resistance, and peaks of clampdown were often followed by increased armed struggle.

Although the British handover of the region to Ethiopia in the 1940s and 1950s was a well-planned process, as far as the transfer of authority between the two occupant authorities was concerned, the situation was different on the ground. From the outset, the second Ethiopian occupation was marred by bloodshed and brutal suppression. The inhabitants of the region could neither comprehend the transfer arrangement, which totally ignored them, nor could they accept the imposition of the occupation, and they therefore rejected the colonial transfer deal. The reaction of the Somali people to the occupation and the consequent loss of freedom, dignity, normal life, etc., was not to surrender but to resist. Spontaneous demonstrations broke out throughout the region when the British handover of the Ogaden to Ethiopia was announced; however, the occupying forces brutally suppressed the uprising.

Although the resistance to the reoccupation began peacefully, Ethiopia responded with brutal military suppression. At the time, organised resistance to the occupation was led by the SYL. The Ethiopians were determined to suppress the national spirit and adherents and sympathisers – the SYL – were particularly targeted. Beginning with the Harar and Dire Dawa, they continued the killing as they occupied the towns one after another.

In 1948, twenty-five SYL members were killed in Jigjiga for protesting against the handover of their land to Ethiopia and for refusing to remove the SYL flag from the headquarters of the organisation. In 1957, seven SYL members were hanged in Jigjiga, and their bodies were displayed in the same town. In 1960, hundreds of innocent people were massacred in and around Aysha for allegedly supporting the SYL and its greater Somalia vision. In 1961, another massacre took place in Dagahbur and the town was burned after some youths hoisted the Somali flag and lowered the Ethiopian flag. Following similar uprisings, Qalafe, Danot, Shilabo and other places were also partially or fully destroyed. In 1963, the Ethiopian army killed two resistance leaders, then cut off their heads and paraded them in Qabridahar. Thousands of people were killed during the period of unrest in 1948-1964.

During the uprising, Haile Selassie tried to legitimise the Ethiopian occupation by establishing clan chiefs, who were intended to mediate between the Ethiopian administrators and the Somali inhabitants. He also attempted to institutionalise the tribute paid by the Somalis to the Ethiopian occupants by introducing, in February 1963, a head tax. In practice, the chiefs were responsible mainly for the collection of the tribute, which the Ethiopians called "tax", and since the chiefs did not exercise any real power, the Somali people were not part of the system. Despite the use of the chiefs in collecting the tribute, the people rejected Haile Selassie's plan and the issue of tribute/tax collection became one of the biggest clash points during the 1960s.

The annexation and the ensuing repression triggered reciprocal resistance, both armed and unarmed. There was consensus among the public on the question of the liberation of the homeland, and the repression reinforced the determination to get rid of the occupiers. Although it was not organised until 1963, the armed resistance intensified, especially after Somalia's independence in 1960, due to the mass killing mentioned above, the tribute demand, the dream of freedom in the region and the continuous repression. A never-ending vicious cycle of violent suppression leading to resistance, which in turn caused more repression and the reciprocal response of increased resistance, became the norm.

After the Ethiopian regime change in 1974, a clampdown ensued and in response, the struggle for freedom was revitalised. A new liberation movement called the Western Somali Liberation Front was established, and that organisation, with help of Somalia, was able to expel the occupants from most of the region in the period 1977-78. However, the liberation did not last long because of an evil alliance led by the Soviet Union, which reversed the victory and took the recently gained freedom from the inhabitants of the region. The reimposition of the occupation had an enormous adverse effect on the living conditions of the population and on peace in the region and beyond.

The invading alliance began its offensive using maximum force and, as they entered the region, they began to kill everyone on sight. The indiscriminate mass killing sent shock waves, which lead to an unprecedented level of internal and external displacement. The havoc of the war, the ensuing massacres and the persistent repression made the region inhospitable. In other words, the war crimes and the resulting psychological, physical and livelihood devastations made the living conditions unbearable and forced most of the inhabitants to flee from the region. Unfortunately, the fleeing refugees were air-bombed by the alliance on the way to neighbouring countries, and many of them perished in that perilous journey.

The most immediate effect of the war was the displacement of the people following the re-conquest of the Ogaden by the Russian-led alliance. The conquering forces bombed towns indiscriminately during the reoccupation campaign and, as a result, the towns were emptied by the inhabitants before the enemy reached them. The displaced people began to move in their tens of thousands eastward, northward and southward toward Somalia and Djibouti, some of them in vehicles, but most of them on foot in search of a safe haven. The Soviet-led alliance, however, was strafing the refugees from the air as they were making their way to the borders. The alliance claimed that they continued the aerial bombing to destroy the capabilities of the fleeing Somali army, but in reality, they did not differentiate between the civilians and the army, and most of those killed were civilians. Other atrocities that followed the reoccupation included the bombing of villages, the massacre of nomads, the poisoning of wells and the killing of livestock.

The Ethiopian government not only admitted the destruction of the towns and the subsequent mass displacement, but ironically, it sought help on behalf of the very people who were fleeing from its bombardment and atrocities. The new commander in the Ogaden, Lemma Gutema, stated that 70 percent of the region had been affected by the war and that most of its small towns had been razed. He estimated the number of displaced persons in the region at one million. The Ethiopian regime appealed for help from the UNHCR in March 1978. Despite the appeal for assistance, Ethiopia refused to allow international observers to enter the Ogaden region to assess the situation of the people it claimed were appealing for their help. Whatever the Ethiopian motive, it became clear from the huge influx of refugees into Somalia that the situation was much worse than the Ethiopian authorities reported.

'According to the Somali government, some 500,000 refugees had arrived within Somalia by May 1978. A further 10,000 refugees were reported to have gone to Djibouti in the same period. During 1978–79, the number of refugees arriving in Somalia continued to grow, and by February 1980 had increased to 600,000. Somalia set up thirty-five refugee camps in four areas of the country. The number of registered refugees in the camps in Somalia was estimated in 1982 at about 700,000 by the UN, but that figure did not include the estimated 600,000 unregistered refugees in the country, who mingled with the local population. By 1981, the number of refugees in Djibouti had reached 45,000. The number of displaced people within the Ogaden was greater than the number of those who had fled to neighbouring countries, and more than 80 percent of the population was affected by the displacement tragedy. Because of the repression that followed the reoccupation, most of the displaced people within the region did not return to their homes for years after the re-conquest.[1]

In Somalia, refugees found a safe haven and were well treated by their Somali brethren until 1991, when the Somali government collapsed, and some refugees were attacked by armed militia. Unlike the refugees in Somalia, the refugees in Djibouti did not get full protection. The bulk of the refugees in Djibouti were forcibly returned to Ethiopia in the 1980s. With the consent of the UNHCR, the governments of Ethiopia and Djibouti carried out the forced repatriation in 1983.

The government of Somalia gave the refugees a safe haven, and the international community generously provided basic necessities to refugees in Somalia, but that was only a temporary solution that could not be sustained in the long run. Therefore, a permanent solution was required to deal with the problem effectively. The huge presence of refugees was a burden to the host country as well as to the donor countries. Also, refugee camps could never be a substitute for their homeland to the refugees. Thus, the sensible thing to do was to identify the basic factors that led to the mass exodus and remove them to ensure the safe return of the refugees to their homeland.

While grateful to the international community for the generous response in assisting the refugees, the government of Somalia always reminded the world body of the need to deal with the source of the mass displacement. The removal of the fundamental causes of the problem would have alleviated the suffering of the refugees, taking the heavy burden of caring for them off the shoulders of the host as well as donor countries, thus making everyone involved better

---

[1] M M Abdi, *A history of the Ogaden (Western Somali) Struggle for Self Determination*, Part I (1300-2007), page 124.

off, and that part of the world a better place to live in. However, attempts by the Somali government to find a resolution at the UN to the refugee crisis by eliminating the root causes of the exodus failed mainly due to the neglect and failures of the international community.

On 9 April 1981, the UNHCR appointed Prince Sadruddin Aga Khan as Special Rapporteur to study the question of human rights and massive exodus. With the appointment of the Special Rapporteur, the refugees' hopes around the world were raised, and the Somalis thought that their calls to deal with the root causes of the refugees' problem had been heeded. However, by the time the report was delivered, it became clear that nothing fundamental was going to change. Because of pressure from Ethiopia and Russia, part of the report including the section about Ethiopian refugees was deleted and the main issue of the root cause of refugees was ignored.

Before the removal of the root causes of their flight, and the government they fled from still in power in Ethiopia, the bulk of Ogaden refugees in Somalia returned home, following the overthrow of the Somali government in 1991 and the subsequent civil war there. Additionally, the region they returned to was experiencing a severe drought, which devastated the main livelihoods of the region, livestock and farming, and led to hunger and starvation. Thus, for the returnees fleeing from the war-torn country, which had hosted them during the 1970s and 1980s, the land they came back to was not home sweet home.

Due to the drought and the lack of a caring government, the region could hardly cope with the overwhelming burden of the huge number of returnees. Despite the indescribable difficulties, the people of the region confronted the reality as they should head on and embarked on rebuilding their lives in whatever way possible.

Against the backdrop of that gloomy situation, the empty-handed returnees began to rehabilitate themselves with the help of the poor local communities, who welcomed them, but the regime change that took place in the same year gave the people of the region new hope. The overthrow of the Mengistu regime in 1991 was a great relief, and the promises of the new government replaced the gloomy situation with cautious optimism.

Amongst other things, the new regime promised respect for the rule of law, observance of human rights, democratisation and the reshaping of the system of government by introducing a federal system. The federal system was intended to deal with the nationality problem, and the new constitution was to give the nations of the republic self-rule and even allow them to secede from the republic if they were not happy to remain part of it.

The new democratic approach from Addis Ababa changed the mood of the population in the Somali Region by changing their long-held pessimism about the attainment of basic human rights and the political development in Ethiopia into one of optimism because none of the aforementioned democratic commitments were imaginable under the previous regimes. In particular, the self-determination promise made the Somali people extremely excited and forward-looking. With unprecedented enthusiasm, they welcomed the new government and cooperated with it fully in maintaining peace and order and made preparations to be part of the new dawn and a democratic Ethiopia, which the new regime claimed to be introducing. The optimism, however, did not last long.

Unfortunately, that hope of a better day soon faded; the new regime came up with some of the usual Ethiopian repression policies before they had finished lecturing about their new democracy. In a short time, the gap between what the new regime proclaimed and its actions on the ground became too big to be reconciled. The new democratic system, which the government claimed to have brought, was accompanied – and even preceded – by the suppression of political parties and indiscriminate killing. To their disappointment, the Somali people in the Ogaden region saw signs of the unpromising reality and what to expect from the Addis Ababa regime before the new regime got full control of the country. However, they had no alternative but to see through the whole deceptive saga unfolding before them.

The EPRDF's nearly three-decade iron rule of the region began with an unprovoked ambush on Al-Itihad in 1992 in which 2 dozen of its members, including the chairman and vice chairman, were killed. The aim of the attack was not only to destroy the party but to unveil the totalitarian nature of its rule and to demonstrate to the dissidents what to expect from the regime. Despite the determination of the EPRDF to disrupt the fragile peace with that show of force, the inhabitants of the region decided to give the desperately needed peace a chance, and for that reason urged Al-Itihad not to respond to the provocation, a call the organisation heeded.

Although it did not take part in the 1992 election, Al-Itihad showed restraint and upheld the ceasefire mediated by the elders of the region. The election was conducted peacefully, and a regional government led by the ONLF was formed. However, the peace did not last long, and the conflict resumed after the democratic process that led to the formation of the regional representative government was reversed. Although the federal government introduced the democratic process that led to the election victory of the ONLF, the result of the election and the overall outcome of the democratic process unnerved it.

On the one hand, the Addis Ababa regime was keen to extract the Ogaden's gas and oil and was not willing to give the owners of the geological resources a say in the running of the business of those resources. On the other hand, the elected assembly and the political parties in the region were adamant about realizing their long dreams of genuine self-rule using the new window of democratisation proclaimed by the EPRDF regime. The proclamation of the introduction of democracy, human rights observance and respect for the rule of law were propaganda messages intended to mislead the people, while consolidating power. All throughout, Ethiopia wanted to utilise the region's resources at the expense of its inhabitants, and that desire to steal the region's natural resources conflicted with the Somali people's aspirations for self-rule and taking control of their resources.

The persistent resistance in the region prevented the Ethiopian regime from benefiting from the exploitation of the Ogaden's natural resources, despite their endless efforts to do so. The inhabitants demonstrated a determination to defend their resources peacefully after the EPRDF took power. The regime noticed the indigenous inhabitants' strong determination and realised that the empowerment of the people through democratisation and the utilisation of the region's geological resources at the expense of the owners were not compatible. For that reason, it decided to end the nascent self-rule experiment and the institutional building processes before it was too late.

The new regime was confident that it would achieve the utilisation of the Somali natural resources without the cooperation of the locals at that juncture because of the dire humanitarian situation in the region and the collapse of the Somali government, which had backed the resistance in the region. For that reason, it closed the door to peace with simultaneous political and military measures to accelerate the exploitation of the Ogaden's gas and oil reserves. To deter dissent, it pre-emptively raided opposition political parties and embarked on a campaign of terror and repression.

The massacre of over eighty civilians at a rally in Wardheer in 1994, the overthrow of the regional administration and the general clampdown that followed were the events that instigated the conflict and set off the armed resistance, which continued until the ousting of the EPRDF regime in 2018.

In the Wardheer attack, the main target was the chairman of the ONLF, who survived. Both Al-Itihad and ONLF were legal parties, and ONLF was even the largest organisation in both the regional government and the assembly when the federal government decided to eliminate them.

From 1994, armed resistance resumed after Ethiopia decided to simultaneously step up the exploitation of the Ogaden geological resources and crush dissenting voices. In that year, Ethiopia requested international financial institutions and donor countries to assist with investment in the gas and oil project in the Ogaden. As mentioned earlier, it got a positive response from the World Bank and the government of the Netherlands. Since then, the exploitation of the geological resources surged and continued with ever-increasing intensity until the overthrow of the regime in 2018. Local opposition to the project reciprocally grew rapidly, and the confrontation culminated in 2007, when opponents to the project took arms to defend their resources. The ONLF stormed an exploration site in Obale operated by a Chinese oil company.

Following the ONLF attack on the Obale site, the crackdown escalated dramatically. Pressured by its partners in the scramble for the Ogaden's natural resources, who were demanding a safe environment conducive to conducting business and still confident that it could crush the opponents to the scramble project, the government embarked on a multidimensional operation consisting of military offensives against the insurgents, civilian crackdowns and dehumanisation acts.

The aim of the operation was not only to suppress the ongoing uprising but to pre-empt any future resistance in any form. The strategies to achieve that goal were twofold: first, the imposition of a scorched earth policy and the instigation of a civil war amongst the indigenous population intended to root out the armed resistance militarily once and for all; and second, the collective punishment of the whole population to force the entire society into submission and thereby deny the resistance a support base and deter the future formation of resistance movements as well.

The strategies and their policy instruments, which were adopted in 2007, were intertwined and complemented one another. For example, the collective punishment of the population and the persecution of the support networks of the rebels were not only the primary means to suppress the voice of general discontent but were also key policy instruments in the operation aimed at the eradication of the insurgents. The impacts of the intertwined strategies of human rights abuses and the scorched earth policy are detailed in part two of the history work entitled 'A History of the Ogaden (Western Somali) Struggle for Self-Determination'. In this book, we summarise the policy measures undertaken by the authorities to quell the rebellion and suppress public discontent and their consequences for the living conditions of the indigenous inhabitants.

In carrying out the first strategy, the government did two things:

it used maximum military force to crush the ONLF army and it turned the conflict into a civil war by the creation of local forces supporting the regular army in the military campaign against the resistance. The latter instrument proved lethal in weakening the resistance because of the division it created within the society and the local expertise that the local forces possessed.

The local enemy, known locally as the Liyu police (Special Police), was recruited entirely from within the indigenous inhabitants who knew the terrain and the support base of the rebels. That local knowledge made their operations more effective than those of the military and because of their ethnic background, the conflict turned into a civil war. The indigenisation of the conflict was further strengthened by giving the responsibility of the collective punishment operations to the local authorities, that is, by making the regional administration responsible for the abuses and delegating the conduct of the crackdown to the local forces.

The combination of the scorched earth policy and the indigenisation of the conflict yielded rapid results for the Ethiopian regime due mainly to the effectiveness of the latter. The rebels lost momentum on the battlefield and lost enthusiasm for the struggle for freedom because of the indigenisation of the war, which cast doubt on the intended purpose of the struggle. The definition of the enemy changed with the appearance of the local militia killing their own people on behalf of the occupants, and the struggle lost its direction because of the two indigenous forces killing one another.

The negative impacts of the second strategy, namely the war against the defenceless population, were more severe than the first strategy because it affected everyone and contributed to the effectiveness of the former. A relentless terror campaign of human rights abuses followed by blockades and livelihood destruction was unleashed in the region in addition to the military assault on the resistance and their supporters.

The methods of the collective punishment of the defenceless civilian population consisted of genocide, widespread arbitrary arrests, mass detention and imprisonment, extrajudicial killings, rape, blockade and the disruption of livelihoods. 'Oppression and state terror were not new to the region as, since the start of the Ethiopian occupation, human rights violations persisted. However, the severity and magnitude of these violations increased dramatically with the new crackdown. The government saw the entire population of the region as backers of the rebel movement, which it was determined to wipe off the face of the earth. By carrying out a crackdown on the whole society and destroying its fundamental livelihood, the government believed that it could achieve victory over these resistance movements'.[1]

Because of the war declarations on the entire society, both the operational area and the targets of the terror campaign were limitless. As part of their daily routine work, each army would attack and round up the people nearest to their location and inflict on them unimaginably harsh punishment, both individually and collectively. The terror campaign spared no one and the punitive measures that were inflicted on the innocent inhabitants, among them the elderly, the sick, women and children included public execution, detention, torture and body dismemberment. Some of the victims were killed on the spot, while others were taken to detention centres and tortured before eventually being killed there or being taken to other prisons.

Due to the frequent armed conflict and the persistent repression in the region, both internal and external displacement were frequent. In the past, most of the displaced people 'fled to the neighbouring countries to escape conflict and repression, but for the survivors of this war, there was nowhere to go—this was because of the blockade Ethiopia imposed on the region and because of Ethiopia's dominance of the Horn. The Ethiopian government closed the borders, and in addition to this, demanded the various regional administrations in Somalia—which it effectively controlled—to return the people fleeing from persecution in the Ogaden region. Ethiopian agents also operated in the whole region of the Horn of Africa and hunted dissidents everywhere in that part of the African

---

[1] M M Abdi, *A history of the Ogaden (Western Somali) Struggle for Self Determination*, Part II (2007–2021), page 11.

continent.'[1]

In addition to the clampdown and the restriction of the movement of the people, the essential goods that the inhabitants depended on, which used to come mainly from Somalia, were barred. All goods and items entering the region without the approval of the army were confiscated. Additionally, the government frequently confiscated harvested crops and livestock or destroyed the crops and killed the animals on the claim that the farmers and the herders supported the resistance.

The combination of these punitive measures turned the region into an open prison, in which the inmates were either liquidated or suffered from starvation and indescribable abuse. Although the human rights abuses took place in different places, such as detention centres, prisons and public and private places, the victims experienced similar harsh treatment everywhere from their first encounter with the perpetrators to the end of their ordeal, which was extermination in many cases.

'Open prisons were the starting point of human rights violations. Here, victims were apprehended, abused and kept until the next phase of their mistreatment. Very often, they would also return to these prisons after the end of their jail terms. These types of prisons were not specific buildings or locations but anywhere people lived their normal lives and carried out their daily routines, such as workplaces, mosques, markets or the local streets. In other words, a whole region could be an open prison'.[2]

Very often, the victims' lives ended where their ordeal began, in the open prison, and if they survived that first stage they would go to the next stage, namely ordinary prison. Some of them were killed on the spot in their first encounter with culprits, and others died of torture or starvation in detention centres. The same perpetrators who oversaw all the punishment places apprehended and abused

---

[1] M M Abdi, *A history of the Ogaden (Western Somali) Struggle for Self Determination*, Part II (2007–2021), page 12.
[2] M M Abdi, *A history of the Ogaden (Western Somali) Struggle for Self Determination*, Part II (2007–2021), Page 23.

their captives wherever they found them. 'The victims could be a father in his home, a shopkeeper in his shop, someone walking down the street, a farmer working on his farm or a herder grazing his livestock on the land. Each one of these victims would encounter the most excruciating abuse on the spot, whether that was psychological, physical, or economical'.[1]

The survivors of that first encounter with the culprits would end up in detention centres, and those who did not perish there would be taken to ordinary jails. Far too many people have been imprisoned in detention centres and jails across the region without committing any crimes and have lived in unthinkable conditions. In both places, the inmates were abused physically, sexually and psychologically. They were starved, humiliated, had no access to medical care and were not allowed to contact their families.

Physically, the prisoners were subjected to unimaginable torture, including beatings, drownings and rape. Some of the routine tortures were water and sewage drowning, where the victims were taken to the water reservoir and the sewage dump often in the middle of the night. They were first tied with their hands and legs together behind their backs. The victims would then be plunged into the water or the sewage upside down. They would be pulled up for a few minutes of interrogation and then pushed down to the water/sewage dump again in the same manner, and such torture would continue for several hours. Daily beating with sticks and water pipes and dragging on hot ash containing the smouldering remnants of firewood or on sewage, burying the victims in wet sand, breaking their limbs, forcing them to eat human excrement, compelling them to stand for days and forcing them to dig their graves prior their murder were some of the routine tortures.

The psychological torture included forced nudity, compulsion to act like an animal or pretending to be mute. Those forced to pretend to be mute or animals were not allowed to talk; instead they had to use sign language or make noises like animals. Another painful and

---

[1] M M Abdi, *A history of the Ogaden (Western Somali) Struggle for Self Determination*, Part II (2007–2021), Page 23.

humiliating torture was ordering men to hold one another's genitals or tying the genitals of men together with a thin rope and forcing them to form a line while naked.

Starvation was by far the most common torture and one of the biggest causes of death in jail. Prisoners often physically changed in a short space of time due mainly to hunger and continual torture. The inmates were not given adequate food and their families were not allowed to bring them food either. The hunger led to the spread of many diseases, and the absence of medical care exacerbated the situation. One after the other, the inmates would lose the ability to stand or walk, and many of them became fully disabled for the rest of their lives. Despite the rapid physical deterioration, death from starvation was slow and that long agony made it a painful death.

The punishments mentioned above by those who gave testimony were common to both sexes. But in addition to that, women were subjected to other severe punishments, which included genital burning, rape, forced impregnation, healthcare deprivation during pregnancy and labour and abuse of their children. Very often, pregnant women would die during labour, and many newborn babies were taken to unknown destinations and most likely sold. There were always children in jails; some of them were born there and others were jailed with their mothers, and no one other than jailed mothers cared for them.

The punishment methods and living conditions in the many prisons across the region were the same. Describing the situation in the infamous prison of Jail Ogaden, one inmate said: 'Jail Ogaden was a place that nobody has ever seen or ever heard the like of before and no human being could ever even imagine'.

As a result of these inhumane treatments and punishments, many of the prison inmates died and many others became disabled. Some of them also lost their reproductive organs because of the severe torture to which they were subjected. They expected death to come to them at any moment, and some of them even wished death to come sooner rather than later and attempted suicide because of their unbearable suffering.

'The main causes of disabilities were beating, burning, being forced to stand for many days and starvation. The prison guards used to beat every part of the victims' bodies, resulting in multi-body dysfunctionality. However, women topped the list of inmates whose internal organs had been damaged by torture. Because of the additional torture, such as gang rape and genital burning, many women lost their reproductive systems. Their kidneys, digestive systems, bowels and other organs became dysfunctional, and they require constant medical care and support to stay alive.'[1]

The people were not only dying slowly in the incarceration centres, but much bigger numbers were machine-gunned in the open prisons as individuals as well as groups. Ethiopia's terror and mass killings were part of the conquest campaign of the Somali Region. The violent occupation was preceded by raids, which resulted in mass killing and looting. After the completion of the annexation, armed suppression was the means to maintain the occupation, which was never accepted and was resisted by the inhabitants of the region. As mentioned in the preceding section, all the successive regimes in Ethiopia waged war against the civilian population and carried out massacres. However, the scale and the frequency of the killing increased dramatically during the EPRDF regime, especially after the Obale battle, which the ONLF launched for the defence of the oil and natural gas in the Somali Region.

Too many massacres took place within the region during the EPRDF reign to describe them all in detail here, and therefore only some of the places where the biggest massacres occurred will be stated. The victims in some of the massacres have been identified, but it was not possible to get a full list of the names of the victims for many incidents, including some of the places in which the biggest massacres occurred. The following is the list of some of them and the number of people killed there.

- Wardheer massacre on 22/2/1994, 81 people were killed and several dozen wounded.

---

[1] M M Abdi, *A history of the Ogaden (Western Somali) Struggle for Self Determination*, Part II (2007–2021), page 56.

- Qabridahar massacre on 15/11/2005, about 30 people were murdered, but the number of wounded is not known.
- Farmadow Massacre 26/10/2005, 7 people were killed and 15 others wounded.
- Shilabo massacre 29/6/2005, 6 people were killed and more wounded.
- Dagahbur 19-21/6/2007, about 30 people were killed and many more wounded.
- Qorile, in July 2007 and in September 2012, over 2 dozen people were murdered in total.
- Mooyaha, on 17/12/2008, 48 civilians were killed and 50 wounded.
- Gunagado, in February 2012, 49 people were killed in various locations within the district.
- Malqaqa in May 2010 over 500 people were killed in the district in a series of mass slaughters.
- Jaama'-Dubad on 5/6/2016, 21 civilians were killed.
- Ela-Obo, in February 2007, 19 people were killed in Ela-Obo in three separate incidents.
- Dagahmadaw, in 2009, 116 people were killed in various locations within the district.
- Aleen: on 29/6/2007, 3 people were killed.
- Gumareey: 23/6/2007, 3 people were murdered.
- Daratoole: 2/6/2007, 6 people were killed.
- Qamuuda: On 25/7/2006, the army summarily executed 5 women.
- Madah-Maroodi: On 15/3/2005, 3 men were killed.
- Karin Bil'illle: On 30/11/2004, 4 people were killed.
- Golhabreed: On 7/4/2004, 2 people were killed.
- Labiga: On 5/3/2001, 7 people were killed.
- Obole: In March 2002, 2 people were killed.
- Garawo: On 27/4/2002, 3 people were executed.

- Nusdariiqa: On 4/2/2003, 5 civilians were murdered.

2.3 Economic Disruption

The bounty of the geological resources was supposed to benefit the inhabitants of the land they lay beneath, but so far, the Somali Region has not seen any economic benefit from the ongoing crude oil and natural gas projects in their state. However, the scramble, the consequent general crackdown and the uprooting of the locals in the Ogaden Basin has had enormous negative impacts on the economy. Government policies designed to enforce the scramble project destroyed the region's subsistence economy directly by disrupting the production of the main livelihoods, and it indirectly reduced the value of its natural energy resources through persistent repression and conflict.

The oil and gas exploration sites are spread throughout the whole of the Ogaden basin, which covers approximately 350,000 square kilometres. Exclusion zones of 30, 50 and 60 kilometres were set up by the government around the areas designated for exploitation, and for that reason, a large population who lived there was forcibly removed from their ancestral land. The uprooting of the local people from their land adversely affected their lives and livelihoods.

The villages where they lived were usually burned after the inhabitants were expelled. With the burning of the villages, the Ethiopian government wiped out the capital and properties of the village dwellers and made them homeless. The creation of exclusion zones further devastated the livelihoods of the displaced people and thereby ruined their living conditions.

The devastating impact of the exclusive zones and the uprooting were not only enormous, but also very quick. 'Farmers and herders have been taken from their lands, which they depended on for everything. Because of the removal from their ancestral land, they have lost both home and livelihood. After the villages they lived in were burned, they were forcibly evicted from their land, thereby making them homeless and displaced in their own country. The loss of agricultural land meant a complete loss of livelihood for these farmers, and the pastoral community's means of living was severely weakened and became unsustainable because of the grazing land they were driven from'.[1]

In addition to the destruction of their livelihoods, these closures led to many life-threatening dangers for herders and their livestock. 'Apart from the loss of grazing land, the lives of both people and animals have come under threat because of the killing of any livestock or human seen in the area by the army. No matter how hard herders try to prevent their livestock from entering closed-off zones, the animals, who do not understand exclusion zones, frequently attempt to move in the direction of the closed-off areas due to overgrazing in other areas, especially during the dry seasons, or because of their habit of going to familiar places. Whenever the animals go near the exclusion zones, the army shoots them on sight, and the herders dare not retrieve them from the danger zones or they will be killed, too. Some animals die from shooting, while others are eaten by predatory animals after fleeing in different directions.'[2]

The negative impacts of the crackdown and the uprooting of the locals on the economy of the region were huge, especially in areas where gas and oil deposits were found. As a result of the village burning, evictions and land closures, the locals lost the homes they had lived in and most of the property they had in the villages. With the loss of their farm and pasture lands, the sources of income of the local community in the Ogaden Basin also disappeared.

Because of the lack of any compensation from the government for the economic tragedy it created and the lack of peaceful places to resettle, the subsequent social and economic devastation of the displaced became permanent. The displaced people 'did not find peace in the places they were expelled to because of the general

---

[1] M M Abdi, *A history of the Ogaden (Western Somali) Struggle for Self Determination*, Part II (2007–2021), Page 92.

[2] M M Abdi, *A history of the Ogaden (Western Somali) Struggle for Self Determination*, Part II (2007–2021), page 90-91.

crackdown that made everywhere in the region unsafe, and in such circumstances, starting a new life became impossible. They become destitute refugees, dependent on food donations, and most of them have been living in feeding centres run by NGOs'.[1]

The uprooting of the locals in the Ogaden Basin prevented pastoralists there from keeping their animals in their ancestral land, the general crackdown prevented them from find alternative farming and pasture lands and the blockades made it impossible for them to find a market where they could sell their livestock. 'Some of the herders tried to change their way of living by selling their livestock, but they failed to do that due to government restrictions. The markets for livestock, which were mainly in neighbouring countries, became out of reach for local herders because of the blockade. The combined punishments made their livelihood unsustainable and prevented them from finding alternative sources of income.'[2]

In addition to the aforementioned adverse effects on the economy, the scramble also negatively impacted the value of the region's natural energy resources. The illegal and violent means the alliance for the scramble for the Ogaden's natural energy resources pursued to grab these resources reduced the value of the resources in several ways.

Interest in the Somali Region's natural resources began in the 19th century when the hunt for oil took centre stage worldwide. However, unlike other parts of the world, where oil companies have sought natural resources legally, they tried to obtain Somali natural energy resources illegally and violently.

After finding traces of petroleum in the second part of the 19th century, the Western oil companies wasted no time trying to get these resources. However, instead of contacting and negotiating with the inhabitants of the region, they allied themselves to a third

---

[1] M M Abdi, *A history of the Ogaden (Western Somali) Struggle for Self Determination*, Part II (2007–2021), Page 93.

[2] M M Abdi, *A history of the Ogaden (Western Somali) Struggle for Self Determination*, Part II (2007–2021), page 93.

party, namely Ethiopia, to get those resources at the expense of the owners. The third party conquered parts of the region prior to the arrival of the oil companies and was contemplating completing the occupation of the whole region. The alliance with oil companies for the scramble for the Ogaden resources not only encouraged Ethiopia to proceed with the annexation plan, but also enabled Ethiopia to accelerate the process of the completion of the occupation.

The plan of the alliance, as expected, provoked a swift reaction from the people whose resources and land were to be misappropriated. Rejecting both the occupation and the embezzlement of their natural resources, they began to resist using all available means. As detailed in the earlier chapters of the book, the conflict that began then has never ended to this day, and has been for the most part an armed conflict. The conflict not only delayed the utilisation of the region's geological resources, but it also reduced the enthusiasm to invest and lowered the value of the resources because of external costs.

The persistent war added a risk cost to all the stages of the exploitation project, thus reducing the profitability of the region's natural resources and thereby reducing the appetite for investment. The oil companies became discouraged by the conflict to invest, and they will take the risk to invest only if they were given exceptional deals above the usual offers for similar projects elsewhere.

Over time, natural resources either lose or gain value because of changes in technology, the discovery of alternative resources or changes related to environmental concerns or consumer preferences. The Somali Region was one of the places where oil was detected at an early stage of the oil boom, and the oil companies started their activities there even before they made deals with many of the oil-rich Gulf states. The oil industry made huge progress in the Gulf states, which changed the economic landscape of the host countries and the countries where the companies originated from and are based. However, because of the illegal and violent approach of the exploitation of the Ogaden's resources, the geological resources of the Somali Region proved to be a source of peril for the region rather than fortune.

The values of the Ogaden's geological resources are always lower because of the risk element, which increases the cost side of the cost/benefit analysis. Additionally, because of the new global environmental concerns, the golden age of oil and gas seems to be over, an opportunity that the Somali Region has lost because of the war initiated by the occupiers and their alliance for the scramble.

Globally, the oil and gas industry has made enormous technological advances since the start of the scramble for natural resources in the Somali region. The technological progress advantage has the potential to reduce the cost of the exploration, extraction and treatment of the resources and also the cost of addressing environmental concerns. However, in the Somali Region, that advantage is offset by the risk cost resulting from the conflict, which in turn is fuelled by the persistent repression and the exclusion of the indigenous inhabitants from the project.

The overall negative impacts of the scramble-driven conflict on the economy, living conditions and the value of the natural resources have been huge. Currently available resources have been adversely affected by the crackdown and the blockade and, so far, the oppressive policies of the government have prevented the utilisation of the geological resources. Despite the government's attempt to utilise the region's geological resources at the expense of the owners, it failed to realise that goal and did not gain anything as a result of the scramble. For the oil companies too, the project was not beneficial, and their investments in the project has so far been wasted. For more than a century, different oil companies have invested in the Ogaden Basin and left before getting any return on their investment. Thus, the overall result of the scramble project is not beneficial to anybody. As outlined above, it has brought only harm to the economy of the Somali Region.

2.4 Health and Environmental Damage

The health of humans in society and other living beings is affected by the environment that surrounds them. Thus, any activity that influences the balance of the habitat ought to be examined carefully before undertaking it to avoid or minimise damage to environmental systems. The expected benefit of the new economic activity should be weighed against the potential environmental damage and its consequences for present and future generations. In other words, environmentally sustainable use of resources and fair distribution of petroleum income amongst the generations are to be ensured.

The oil and gas project in the Ogaden Basin has huge ramifications for the environment in the region and will have consequential health impacts. The ongoing and planned exploration activities cover nearly the whole region, and that wide geographical coverage makes the impacts on the ecological balance widespread. Since human society and other living organisms depend on the environment, any damage to the habitat will have an impact in both the short and long term. Because of the magnitude of health and environmental consequences, a responsible and caring government would have made collaborative assessments and arrangements with the locals to deal with all the existing and potential environmental stresses and health repercussions before undertaking a project of this type and magnitude.

Unfortunately, the government's policies and actions regarding these issues have not conformed with what is expected of responsible authorities. It seems the primary goal of the Ethiopian government and its partners in the scramble project is to extract natural gas and crude oil at any cost and thus environmental assessments, livelihood assessments and the impact on health are not part of their agenda, or at least not their main concerns.

'Usually, when the army completes Somali ethnic cleansing through killing, displacement and the burning of villages, the foreign oil companies begin the destruction of the environment bit by bit, starting with the cutting down of trees and removing of grassy pastures and ending the clearing work by creating empty spaces to conduct exploration and extraction activities of crude oil and natural gas. The consequent deforestation and subsequent exploration and extraction destroy the habitat and turn large green areas into permanent deserts.'[1]

The deforestation is obvious, but other environmental damage is not documented by the indigenous communities because of their exclusion from the project. The 700-900-kilometre pipeline from the Ogaden Basin to Djibouti will certainly lead to further deforestation if its construction is carried out as planned. Both the extraction points and the pipeline pose potential environmental risks, such as fuel spills and other environmental degradations, including soil erosion, water contamination and air pollution, and the inhabitants of the Basin are already suffering from some of the health consequences of the project.

The health and environmental consequences that have already affected the lives and livelihoods of the inhabitants are indicative of the looming ecological dangers. A mystery disease first reported in 2014 by the locals came to light in the public domain in 2020, when a leading British newspaper published an article about the disease. The Guardian newspaper published in February 2020 a detailed story about the possible origins of the disease, its symptoms, its fatality rate, and its severe health impacts on the communities.

The symptoms, which include a swollen body, yellow or green eyes and palms, bleeding from the mouth and nose, teeth and hair falling out, insomnia and fever, indicate a serious disease that's new to the region. The affected communities have also reported unprecedented miscarriages from pregnancy, birth defects, cancer and psychological problems that were not seen in the area before the disease.

The outbreak of the illness not only coincided with the arrival of POLY-GCL to the region, but the company also admitted to some chemical spills, which it claimed had happened accidentally during transportation. Additionally, the area where the chemical spills occurred is where the disease was first discovered and the toll from the illness was highest. Although one cannot rule out the possibility of other factors that might have causal or aggravating effects on the

---

[1] M M Abdi, *A history of the Ogaden (Western Somali) Struggle for Self Determination*, Part II (2007–2021), page 93.

disease, the correlation between the activity of the exploitation and the mystery disease, which is so far confined to the exploitation area, is evident.

Whatever the cause, the reported disease poses serious health issues for present and future generations. The sensible thing to do in a situation like this is to first dispatch a medical relief team to the area, followed by an independent and competent investigation into the causes of the illness. Instead, the government sent an investigation team made up of government officials and headed by the Ministry of Mines and Petroleum, after denying the existence of the disease. The government's team confirmed the predeclared position of the government. The apparent correlation between the disease and the scramble project and the government's response to the unfolding health disaster clearly indicate a cover-up attempt by the authorities of the apparent calamity.

Despite the admission of wrongdoing, the Chinese company that was operating in the area did nothing to rectify the damage to the environment and the health of the indigenous communities suffering from the disease or other environmental damage related to the project. Furthermore, the government seems determined to suppress anything that reveals the ugly face of the oil and gas project. The irresponsibility of the oil companies and the government's lack of interest to find a remedy for the health disaster has further aggravated the situation.

The present situation is unsustainable, and the status quo must change before things get out of hand. Important issues such as health and environment cannot be left to irresponsible agents, whose main aim is to deplete the natural resources and who do not care about the environment or the rightful owners of the natural energy resources. A change in attitude toward these issues followed by prompt action on the ground is needed first and foremost. The government's lack of interest in the environment and the lives and well-being of the primary stakeholders and the latter's absence from the project must end, and the host communities must have a say in all the phases and facets of the project.

3

The Impacts of the Scramble Beyond the Somali Region

3.1 Horn of Africa Conflicts

The conquest of the Somali Region for ownership of its geological resources has not only made that region a war zone, but it has also led to armed confrontations in the wider Horn of Africa region. The scramble for the geological resources of the Ogaden is one of the main root causes of Ethiopia's conflict with Eritrea and Somalia.

After signing an oil and exploration deal on 7 September 1945 with the Ethiopian Emperor, Haile Selassie, the American oil company Sinclair wrote a letter on 27 September 1945 to the then US Secretary of state, James F. Byrnes, asking him to back Haile Selassie's efforts to federate Eritrea with Ethiopia. Finding an export outlet for the Ogaden's gas and oil was the sole reason behind the request. Eritrea was federated with Ethiopia in 1952 with help of the US government due largely to the oil and gas issue of the Ogaden and the promise of a military base in Eritrea to the Americans by Haile Selassie.

The incorporation of Eritrea into Ethiopia for the main purpose of getting having a port for the export of the Ogaden oil and gas and the consequent conflict between Eritrea and Ethiopia gravely impacted the peace and stability in the Horn of Africa. After a liberation struggle that lasted 30 years, Eritrea gained independence in 1993.

The Eritrean war caused a huge loss of human life, big destruction of materials and the displacement of many people. We are not covering here the details of that war and its impacts on the Horn as they are recorded elsewhere. However, it is worth mentioning that the conflict between the two nations did not end, despite the independence of Eritrea. The two countries fought a bloody war in the period 1998-2000 over a border dispute and were technically at war until the 2019 peace agreement in which Ethiopia agreed to hand over the disputed area to Eritrea.

Furthermore, the Tigray region, which claims the disputed land area, did not accept the peace deal and thus the agreement is ineffective. The current dispute between the Ethiopian region of Tigray and Eritrea, which originated from the incorporation of Eritrea into Ethiopia and that in turn resulted largely from the scramble for the Ogaden's geological resources, is one of the most difficult conflicts in the Horn. The personal rivalry between the elites of the two sides further exacerbated that conflict.

The scramble affected the whole of the Horn region, but perhaps its impacts on the relationship between Ethiopia and Somalia are not only the most publicised but also the most far-reaching. The two countries have fought over the Ogaden issue politically and militarily for many years and have not reached a permanent agreement over that conflict, despite the cease in the hostilities. The following is a brief account of that confrontation.

As mentioned in chapter 2, the occupation, the ensuing repression and the scramble for the natural resources of the Ogaden sparked outrage, which promptly developed into a general uprising. The subsequent violent suppression of the opposition and the outrageous human rights violations further widened the discontent and ignited a resistance campaign. The resistance that began in the Ogaden right after the conquest never ended, despite periodical respites for revitalisation or due to events related to regime changes.

The conflict has been primarily between the inhabitants of the region and the occupants; however, the Somali inhabitants were supported by Somalia in their pursuit to remove the occupants. As retaliation for that support, Ethiopia waged wars on the Somali republic, undertook destabilisation measures against it and worked hard to destroy Somalia.

After clashes with a local resistant movement known as Nasrullah, Ethiopia attacked Somalia in 1964 to divert attention from the real issue of colonisation and turn the conflict into a border dispute between Ethiopia and Somalia, in which the latter would be portrayed as the aggressor. In achieving that goal of cause misrepresentation, Ethiopia embarked on a diplomatic campaign, involving the promotion of a resolution for the African continent regarding the colonial borders, taking a leadership role in the shaping of the continental organisation, the Organisation of African Unity (OAU), which later changed its name to African Union (AU), and the isolation of its rival neighbour.

The European colonisers divided the African continent among themselves and in total disregard for nationality, ethnicity and cultures. They drew border lines that divided nations, communities and families. In the establishment process of the OAU, Ethiopia convinced the African leaders to preserve the provisional borders of the continent drawn by the colonial powers for the sake of the unity of the OAU member states. Haile Selassie argued that there are too many border disputes to resolve, and the unity of the organisation would not be achieved unless the border disputes were ignored. The prioritisation of the unity of the organisation was a sellable argument, which most of the African leaders promptly accepted.

Ethiopia cunningly sought to legitimise the territories it conquered during the scramble for Africa by presenting them as part of the wider border disputes created by the colonial demarcation, and the acceptance of the African leaders of the preservation of the colonially set borders boosted the Ethiopian position. That border compromise was key to the Ethiopian achievements in the legitimation process of its conquered territories. It also enabled Ethiopia to strengthen its standing in the continent.

Following that first diplomatic achievement, which the Ethiopian regime gained through African solidarity propaganda, and which was instrumental in the legitimisation process of the lands it occupied, Ethiopia took further steps in taking the driving seat of the organisation. Ethiopia hosted the inauguration conference of the OAU, which was held in Addis Ababa in May 1963, and during that conference it also requested that the African leaders make

Addis Ababa the headquarters of the organisation, a request that was granted. After gaining broad support from the African leaders for the retention of the colonial borders as well as recognitions of statesmanship from his fellow leaders, Haile Selassie began the next step of isolating Ethiopia's main opponent, namely Somalia, using the newly established organisation and its resolution on colonial borders.

The diplomatic tricks that Ethiopia employed in misrepresenting the just cause of the Ogaden had two intertwined strategies. The first step was to promote continental rules in dealing with colonial borders, and the second step was to reframe the colonial question and present it as a border dispute between two sovereign countries. Ethiopia seized the right moment to promote its own territorial interests during the establishment of the OAU and made considerable progress in achieving its territorial goals in the first phase of the formation processes. The OAU's adoption of article III paragraph 3 in 1963 and the 1964 Cairo declaration sealed that diplomatic victory. Using Article III paragraph 3 of the OAU charter, which demands respect for the sovereignty and territorial integrity of each state, and the Cairo declaration in which the OAU declared that colonial borders would not be altered to reflect on-the-ground realities regarding ethnicity, language or religion, Ethiopia presented the Ogaden cause as a border dispute and accused Somalia of violating that article.

Despite Ethiopia's successful diplomacy, the situation remained unaltered on the ground. The inhabitants rejected the Ethiopian claim over their land as well as the misrepresentation of their cause. Thus, the conflict continued unaffected by the Ethiopian attempts to hide the colonial question behind the facade of African unity, and the charter declarations of the OAU did not deter the determination of the Somali people to fight for their rights.

On the contrary, the Ethiopian move to legitimise the conquered land through the OAU charter and the subsequent suppression of the anti-colonial uprising ignited the conflict. The armed resistance resumed under the leadership of the WSLF, which replaced the Nasrullah movement, and the war intensified in the 1970s following

Somalia's liberation war and the consequent intervention of the Soviet alliance, which supported Ethiopia.

Somalia took part in the 1977-78 Ogaden war in which most of the Somali Region was liberated. However, that Somali victory did not last long. The Eastern bloc countries did not only rescue the tyrannical regime in Addis Ababa, but also reimposed the Ethiopian occupation of the Somali Region. The atrocious regime, which the Eastern alliance reinstated in the Somali Region, drove the bulk of the inhabitants of the region from their homes and made them either internally displaced or refugees in the neighbouring countries.

Following the defeat of the Somali forces by the Eastern alliance, Ethiopia embarked on aggressive military attacks on the republic of Somalia after the war. The Ethiopian air force frequently carried out air bombardment on Somali cities and towns, bombing and strafing the inhabitants indiscriminately. Ethiopian troops also invaded Somalia several times, capturing some towns. Apart from the human and material losses caused mainly by the air bombardment, the Ethiopian military aggression was not successful as the invading army was repulsed by the Somali army, but the destabilisation policies that the successive Ethiopian regimes pursued against Somalia afterwards proved effective.

After the 1977-78 war, Ethiopia systematically undertook destabilisation measures against the Somali Republic. Initially, the aim was to bring down the Somali regime, but since the collapse of that regime, the goal has been the prevention of the return of effective central government. It used rebel movements that it trained and armed as the tool to achieve both goals, a tool that proved useful for the purpose.

'The armed opposition contributed to the decline of the Somali state in two ways. First, they divided the population along clan lines, and thereby undermined the unity of the nation. They replaced the national aspiration with a tribal one and aroused hostile sentiments among the various clans. In other words, they exchanged the national identity for clan identity and gradually destroyed the identity of the Somali nation. The other way they contributed to the destruction was by their surrender to the Ethiopians. Through them,

Ethiopia got access to valuable classified information about the Somali nation, its make-up and its army, and because of their collaboration, Ethiopia was able to penetrate deep into the Somali state and manipulate Somali politics. The latter, which the Somali armed groups provided to Ethiopia, became particularly useful leverage that Ethiopia still possesses and effectively uses.'[1]

Ethiopian-backed rebel movements ousted the Somali regime in 1991, and the country plunged into a civil war because of the failure of the rebel movements to form a government to replace the deposed regime. Ethiopia took advantage of the chaotic situation and fuelled the civil war using the rebel movements that removed the central authority and instigated the civil war. The Ethiopian government not only fuelled the civil war, but its forces invaded Somalia several times on the pretext of combating terrorism or aiding a warlord allied to it.

In December 2006, it launched a full-scale war on Somalia and occupied many parts of the country, including the capital, to oust the newly established Islamic Courts administration. The Islamic Courts made big headway in restoring law and order in the country and was in the process of establishing an effective central government, but that development did not please Ethiopia. For that reason, the Ethiopian regime decided to eliminate the organisation and thereby prevent the restoration of a central authority in Somalia. It succeeded to oust the organisation and continued to manipulate the politics and the security of Somalia until the fall of the EPRDF regime in 2018.

Due to the regime change in Ethiopia in 2018 and the subsequent civil war there, Ethiopia's destabilisation activities in Somalia subsided to some extent, but Ethiopia's geopolitical goals are unchanged, and Somalia is still a divided country. The threat to deepen the fragmentation of the Somali society and the capability it demonstrated in carrying out that threat is Ethiopia's main leverage over Somalia.

---

[1] M M Abdi, *A history of the Ogaden (Western Somali) Struggle for Self Determination*, Part I (1300-2007), Page 139.

The Ethiopian government wanted to protract the civil war in Somalia and worked hard to prevent the return of a strong central government. To pre-empt its perceived threats from Somalia and cover up the issue of the Ogaden, it made relentless efforts to shift the battlefield from the Ogaden to Somalia. It succeeded in destabilising Somalia but was not able to bury the Ogaden cause, which was the ultimate goal of that strategy.

Despite the current relative calm between Ethiopia and Somalia due mainly to the domestic difficulties each of them is facing and the relative peace in the Ogaden, the central issue remains unresolved and thus the fire is burning under the ashes. In addition to that, the joining of Djibouti in the scramble for the geological resources of the region has further widened the scope and the impact of the Ogaden conflict on the Horn of Africa.

The recent Djibouti and Ethiopian agreement on the utilisation of the Ogaden geological resources has added a new layer to the Horn of Africa's central conflict issue, namely the Ogaden issue. The alliance between Ethiopia and Djibouti, a country with a Somali majority, for the scramble for the geological resources of the Somali Region is a new phenomenon that breaks with the historical Somali solidarity attitude and sharply contrasts with the collective campaigns of the Somali people that underpinned the liberation efforts of the Somali territories, including Djibouti.

Through the Somali warlords, Ethiopia succeeded in toppling the Somali central government, in preventing the return of effective central government and in turning the save havens in Somalia for those fleeing from Ethiopian prosecution into detention centres under the supervision of Ethiopian agents and from which it frequently kidnapped victims and took them back to Ethiopia. The new threat from Djibouti to its Somali brethren in the Ogaden further weakened the defence against Ethiopian aggression, but it is unlikely to affect the determination of the indigenous inhabitants of the Somali Region to defend their resources and strive for independence.

3.2 Superpowers' Geopolitical Conflicts

If you were surprised how the geological resources underneath that tiny piece of semi-desert land in the Horn of Africa attracted the wealthiest nations on the Earth, you will be further astonished by how the conflict over the nomads' backyard has affected major decisions on disarmament and world peace. Confrontations between the US and USSR over the Horn of Africa have had dire consequences for the Horn of Africa region and had profound effects on the relationship between the two superpowers and disarmament. Additionally, the competition between the US and the rising superpower China over the natural energy resources of the Ogaden and over the dominance of the Horn has already led to tension between the two countries, though the fluid situation in the region resulting from internal conflicts and instability in both Ethiopia and Somalia has disoriented them to some extent, and the wait for the outcome of the internal conflicts to some extent reduced the pace of the competition between the US and China.

In the previous sections, we briefly mentioned some of the consequences of superpower intervention in the Ogaden, such as the internal displacement, refugee crises, human rights abuses, as well as Ethiopia's destabilisation policies in Somalia and the subsequent civil war there. In this section, we will summarise how the Ogaden conflict has affected the relationship between the Eastern and Western alliances and world peace. Additionally, the impacts of China's hunt for the Ogaden geological resources and its drive to make the Horn a Chinese client, on the Ogaden resistance to the occupation and on the scramble, as well as on the great powers' geopolitical infighting in the Horn, will be discussed.

Since the 16th century, the Western European powers and Russia have been active in the Horn region, and all supported Abyssinia in its confrontations with its neighbours. However, the friendship treaties of 1953 and 1974 between Ethiopia and the USA and the Soviet Union and Somalia, respectively, formally put Ethiopia in the Western camp and Somalia on the Soviet side, and the showdown in the Horn between the Western and Eastern alliances, led by the

USA and the Soviet Union, began in earnest during the middle of the 1977-78 Ogaden war.

The superpowers' involvement in the Ogaden conflict began with clashes between Ethiopia and Somalia over the Ogaden issue in the 1960s and took centre stage during the 1970s. Following the 1964 war between Ethiopia and Somalia in which the US government not only supported the Ethiopian position on the conflict but also armed the Ethiopian forces to the teeth, Somalia sought Soviet assistance and eventually made a friendship agreement with the Soviet Union in 1974, primarily to get military assistance and superpower patronage.

Neither the Soviet Union nor the US supported the Somali dreams of taking back the Ogaden region that Ethiopia had conquered. In addition to that, both the US and the Soviet governments assisted Ethiopia militarily in its confrontation with the resistance in the Ogaden region. Despite their support for Ethiopia, both countries wanted to have good relations with Somalia on condition that Somalia accepted some sort of settlement over the Ogaden question within an Ethiopian context.

Since the 1953 Ethio-US friendship treaty until the abrogation of that treaty in 1977, Ethiopia was the biggest recipient of US military assistance in Africa. In fact, Ethiopia got over half of the military aid America gave to the whole of Africa. In addition to a huge amount of military equipment, which included aircraft and tanks, a large number of Ethiopian forces were trained in the USA.

All in all, American military assistance was enormous during the rule of Haile Selassie and especially after the Ogaden war. 'American military influence was most evident in the fields of training and equipment. US military aid in the period between 1946 and 1972 came to over $180 million. Over 2,500 Ethiopians underwent diverse forms of military training in the United States between 1953 and 1968. The jet aircraft, anti-tank and anti-aircraft weapons, naval craft, infantry weapons and sometimes even the uniforms were of American origin. In both equipment and training, the air force remained the most prestigious showpiece of American military aid in Ethiopia. It was also reputedly the most modern and efficient unit of the armed forces.'[1]

Because of its desire to spread its socialist ideals, increase its influence in the world and get a foothold in the Horn region, the USSR agreed to give Somalia the military assistance it requested. 'During the 1960s the Soviet Union provided Somalia with a substantial number of T-34 tanks, armoured personnel carriers, MiG 15 and MiG 17 aircraft, small arms and ammunition. After the signing of the 1974 Treaty of Friendship, the Soviet Union increased its military assistance to Somalia. The military hardware Somalia received from the Soviet Union during the 1970s included 50 MiG 21 jet fighters, a squadron of 11–28 bombers, 150 T-35 and 100 T-54 tanks, a SAMA-2 and a modern torpedo and missile-armed fast attack and landing craft for the navy. By the time the Soviets were expelled from Somalia in 1977, about 2,400 Somali military personnel had undergone training in the Soviet Union and another 150 in Eastern Europe. About 3,600 Soviet advisers were stationed in Somalia to train the Somali army and other government workers.'[2]

The Soviets did not support Somali territorial claims, but they wanted to strengthen the Somali position to force Ethiopia to a negotiated settlement sponsored by the Soviet Union over the Ogaden issue and thereby extend Soviet influence throughout the Horn region. After the overthrow of Haile Selassie in 1974, the new military regime in Ethiopia turned to the East, and as result, the relationship between Ethiopia and the Eastern alliance improved. However, the Soviet attempt to bring both Ethiopia and Somalia into the Soviet sphere of influence and resolve the Ogaden issue within a socialist framework failed because of the persistent Somali demand for the independence of the Ogaden region. As the war progressed and it became clear to the Soviet Union that it could not keep both clients, it chose Ethiopia and dumped Somalia.

Following the shift of client alignment, 'the Soviets halted all

---

[1] Bahru Zewde, 1991, *A History of Modern Ethiopia (1855–1974)*, James Currey, page 186.

[2] M M Abdi, *A history of the Ogaden (Western Somali) Struggle for Self Determination*, Part I (1300-2007), page 90-91.

THE IMPACTS OF THE SCRAMBLE BEYOND THE SOMALI REGION

military aid to Somalia and began to supply arms to Ethiopia. Many Soviet military advisers went straight from Somalia to Ethiopia, even taking with them virtually all the Somali maps of the region. From May 1977 through March 1978, by land and by sea, the Soviet Union supplied about $1.5 billion in military equipment to Ethiopia. This represented more than seven times the military aid that the Soviets had supplied to Somalia during the previous three years.'[1]

The Soviet alliance not only provided Ethiopia with a massive amount of military hardware, but it fully participated in the war at all levels, militarily, diplomatically, and so on. The Eastern alliance wanted to end the war quickly to avert the internationalisation of the conflict and the possible involvement of the UN Security Council. The Soviets were especially keen to achieve swift victory to raise their standing in the world and thereby strengthen their negotiating position regarding détente and arms control negotiations. To achieve these intertwined goals, the Soviets airlifted to Ethiopia tens of thousands of Cuban and south Yemeni combat troops as well as thousands of Soviet and Eastern European army experts in addition to the massive amount of military equipment.

Although the superpowers armed Somalia and Ethiopia, they were reluctant to join the fighting at the beginning, and both of them tried to have good relations with the conflicting sides. But as the war progressed, the Soviet-led alliance joined the fighting to rescue the beleaguered Ethiopian regime and defeat its former ally. That Soviet intervention instigated the superpower confrontations over the Horn, which led to the demise of détente and specifically the termination of the strategic arms control agreement known as SALT II. In 1974, Leonid Brezhnev and President Gerald Ford signed in Vladivostok a joint communique on the Strategic Arms Limitation Talks (SALT II). But the agreement was cancelled because of a change of approach in the US engagement with the Soviet Union, which in turn was caused by the USSR intervention in the Ogaden war.

---

[1] David D. Laitin & Said S. Samatar, 1987, *Somalia, A Nation in Search of a State*, Westview Press, Page 142.

Détente was intended to reduce tension between the United States and the Soviet Union and covered a host of issues, which included arms race control, trade, the division of Europe and the competition for the third world. The two countries had an understanding on the issues concerning Europe and arms race control, but not on the third world issues. The Soviet Union wanted to be recognised as an equal power in the world and for the Soviets, détente was the tool to demonstrate that desired position, whereas the US saw détente as a means to influence Soviet behaviour and a control mechanism to limit the expansion of socialism in the third world. Disagreements over the handling of several third-world crises heightened the tension between the two countries and brought the conflict over the third world to the limelight. Lack of understanding of how to resolve conflicts in several places, such as Chile, the Middle East and Angola, led to frustration on both sides and raised the stakes of the competition and the confrontation between the two sides. But it was the Ogaden war that set off the confrontation between the superpowers.

Although the US government supported the Ethiopian position on the Ogaden issue, the Soviet friendship with Ethiopia and the need to contain the Eastern bloc's expansion forced it to act as patron to Somalia. The US position on the Ogaden issue did not change with the change of client and the US administration refused to give Somalia military equipment equivalent to what the Soviets provided to Ethiopia. Nevertheless, it replaced the Soviet Union as the ally of Somalia to counteract the aggressive expansion of the Soviet Union.

The Ogaden war and the resulting shift of alliances affected the US-Soviet bilateral relations in several ways. Both countries tried relentlessly to increase their influence in the Horn region at the expense of the other. The Soviets saw the conflict as an opportunity to expand communism and wanted to add the American regional ally (Ethiopia) to the Soviet camp and thereby make the US friendless in the Horn. Despite the left-leaning tendency shown by the military regime in Ethiopia and the regime's rejection of the American conditions for continued friendship, of which improvement of the human rights situation and a peaceful approach to the Eritrean conflict were the most important ones, the Carter administration did not stop the arms supply to Ethiopia for fear of losing it to the Soviets. The Soviets also tried hard to keep both Somalia and Ethiopia in the socialist alliance, but when the Soviets realised that they could not keep both countries, they dumped Somalia and supported Ethiopia to defeat the former. The US could not swallow the arrogant behaviour shown by the Soviets in this conflict and decided to counteract their designs in the region. The result was a shift of alliances and a new approach to American and Soviet relations.

The Soviet intervention in the Horn opened a new chapter of competition between the two superpowers and made the Horn a major Cold War hotspot. On the one hand, the Soviets were adamant to use military power to assert their power and outmanoeuvre their opponent, and on the other hand, the US government not only disapproved of the military approach that the Soviet Union espoused for the resolution of the Ogaden conflict, but it also could not accept the active Soviet support for the spread of communism into the Third World. As a result of the standoff in the Horn, progress on the other issues of détente came to a standstill. 'Specifically, the crisis undermined the key project of arms control discussions, leading President Jimmy Carter's National Security Advisor, Zbigniew Brzezinski to claim that "SALT lies buried in the sands of the Ogaden."'[1]

That famous phrase of Brzezinski was indicative of the new American approach regarding the East and the West relations and the demise of détente. Washington used the conflict in the Horn to test whether it could force Moscow to play by its rules. Its inability to do so signalled to the United States that détente had failed. The fallout from this manifested itself in a renewed Cold War on both sides, which again played out to the detriment of the third world.

The new American administration led by Jimmy Carter initially

---

[1] Louise Woodroofe, *"Buried in the Sands of the Ogaden"*, *The United States, the Horn of Africa and the Demise of Détente*, The Kent State University Press 2013, page 7.

had faith in the workability of détente, but the events that unfolded in the Horn during the 1977-78 Ogaden War quickly changed that optimism into disappointment, and as a result, American foreign policy towards the East was redirected from détente to containment. Following the policy shift, the Carter administration withdrew SALT II from the Senate, and that pull-out formally ended détente.

Because of the end of détente, the Cold War sentiment resumed in full force. The American foreign policy took a new course, changing Washington's relations with Moscow from one of conciliation to one of confrontation. The Soviet invasion of Afghanistan in 1979 further exacerbated the conflict. The position of the United States towards the communist bloc hardened after the election of Ronald Reagan in 1981 and the relationship between the East and West remained tense until Mikhail Gorbachev took power in the Soviet Union in 1985.

Although the superpowers determined the outcome of the Ogaden war, they were dragged into the conflict by their regional allies, who took advantage of the superpower rivalry and their competition for supremacy in the Horn. In other words, the clients set the political agenda in this conflict by instigating the war and pressing the superpowers to take sides in the conflict.

Other factors, such as human rights issues and trade, might have played part in the demise of détente, but the Ogaden conflict, which resulted from the occupation and the subsequent scramble for its natural resources, was the main cause for the failure of détente and the consequent end of arms race control. The Ogaden war directly affected the bilateral relations of the superpowers and hence changed the course of their foreign policies.

The superpower intervention had devastating consequences for the Horn, especially for the Somalis, both in the Ogaden and Somalia, as briefly outlined in previous sections. The war ended with the restoration of the occupation, dashing once again the hopes of the freedom fighters in the Ogaden to get rid of the yoke of the invaders. The fallout from Soviet intervention was detrimental to the statehood of the Somali Republic. The instability, the collapse of the central government and the subsequent civil war that took place in Somalia were all related to the Somali defeat, which the Soviet intervention caused.

The Soviet Union was given exploration rights of the Ogaden geological resources as a reward for their military support, which brought about the Ethiopian victory, as was the case with Americans when they helped Ethiopia with the reoccupation of the Ogaden after the Second World War. The Soviet oil company, the Soviet Petroleum Exploration Expedition (SPEE), was given exploration and development rights. The company picked up the work from where the American companies left it, developing further what they had discovered and making successful exploration surveys in new areas in the Ogaden Basin. But like the American companies, the SPEE was forced to leave the region before extracting the natural energy resources because of regime change in Ethiopia.

Despite the victory of the Soviet-led alliance, the struggle for freedom continued and the issue of the natural resources became a central battle ground due to the globalisation and intensification of the scramble. After the regime change in Ethiopia in 1991, the new regime invited companies from all over the world to explore the Ogaden for geological resources. As mentioned in chapter 1, most of the foreign companies pulled out from the oil and gas project one after the other for security reasons, and the withdrawal brought the scramble project to a standstill.

In an attempt to revive the stalled project, the then Ethiopian premier, Meles Zenawi, visited China in 2012. During the visit, the two countries made a deal in which China was given the main contract for the exploration and development of the Ogaden oil and gas in exchange for an economic assistance package. With that deal, China, the rising superpower, inherited the gas and oil project in the Ogaden Basin, which was begun by US companies and expanded by the Soviet Union company.

As mentioned in chapter 1, the Chinese company POLY-GCL held the main contract of the project until recently, and according to the crapped tripartite (Ethiopia, POLY-GCL and Djibouti) agreement, the currently available gas would be transported through a pipeline to a Djibouti port, where it would be developed into liquefied natural gas (LNG) and from there, the LNG would be exported to China. However, POLY-GCL's contract was revoked before work on the pipeline and the construction of the treatment plant in Djibouti started.

The Ethiopian government wants to revive the stalled project once again and is expected to invite international oil companies to compete for the takeover of the project. However, the reactivation of the project is unlikely to commence soon due to the civil war in Ethiopia, the geopolitical competition in the Horn, the unpredictable outcome of the fluid political situation in the Horn and above all the lack of consent from the real owners of the resources, namely the Somali people.

A civil war with multiple fronts is ongoing in several parts of Ethiopia, of which the northern conflict is the biggest. Initially, that northern conflict broke out as a result of a political standoff between the Tigray regional authority and the federal government, but because of land disputes between that region and its northern and western neighbours, namely Eritrea and the Amhara region, the neighbours entered the war to support the Ethiopian government army in order to seize the disputed territories they claimed. In addition to these three fronts, the Tigray fighters opened a new front by invading the Afar region, which lies to the east of Tigray. The northern war is ongoing on all four fronts, though the fighting is concentrated on the Amhara region for the time being. The Oromo Liberation Army is also waging a war against the central government in several areas within the Oromo region, and there are interregional conflicts in some other parts of the country.

Although POLY-GCL held the main contract of the Ogaden gas and oil project, other competitors have been knocking on the door to get a portion of the cake or to replace the Chinese company. The competitors include US and UAE companies.

The US government is not happy about the heavy involvement of China in Ethiopia, and especially the takeover by a Chinese company of the Ogaden gas and oil project, which American companies started. In a new move apparently linked to the civil war in Ethiopia, some Congressional representatives met with Somali regional diaspora community members, who briefed them about the mysterious sickness alleged to have been caused by chemical waste dumped on the ground by POLY- GCL, as well as the other negative impacts of the project.

The lobby group Von Batten-Montague-York, L.C. was instrumental in taking the issue to the Congressional representatives. The Somali diaspora group that represented the region in the meeting got also support from associates of the Tigray Peoples Liberation Front (TPLF), who acted as an intermediary between Von Batten-Montague-York, L.C. and the Somali community.

It was the TPLF-led EPRDF government that gave the contract to the Chinese company, and the US government supported that regime in defeating the resistance that had defended the region's geological resources. Additionally, the US government ignored the mystery disease issue when the international press reported it in 2020. Out of rivalry with China and because of its disagreements with Ethiopia over the Tigray crisis, parts of the US political establishment seem to have suddenly changed their position regarding the issue of the Ogaden's energy resources, as indicated by the keen interest they showed in knowing about the link between the mystery disease and the activities of POLY-GCL in the Ogaden Basin. The Tigray interest in this case at this juncture was to widen the conflict and get a helping hand from the Somali Region to oust the current regime.

Both the US and China have military bases in Djibouti. The two countries also have strong strategic interests in Ethiopia and the Horn region. Besides that, the American and Chinese bases are to some extent linked to the geological resource scramble in the Ogaden and the geopolitical goals of the two countries in the Horn.

The US army in Africa, known as AFRICOM and based in Djibouti, aided the Ethiopian army and closely cooperated with the Ethiopian security authorities. AFRICOM paid frequent visits to the Ogaden region during the reign of the EPRDF, officially for anti-terror-related matters; however, their mission was not, as they claimed, only a counter-terrorism operation. The Americans did not support the liberation fronts fighting for their freedom and the protection of their resources from the looters. On the contrary, the US government was the main backer of the Ethiopian government in its fight against rebels in the Ogaden. However, the Americans did not condemn the resistance's military operations against the Chinese oil companies operating in the region.

The Chinese military base at Doraleh in Djibouti is the first Chinese military base outside its territory. Although China claims to have established it for the protection of its commercial vessels passing through the Bab El-Mandeb strait from pirates, the timing, and the heavy involvement of China in Ethiopia after the establishment of the base, suggest a link between the Ogaden gas project and the base. The base was established in 2017 after the attack on the Chinese exploration facility in Obale in which 9 Chinese workers were killed, and after POLY-GCL signed a long-term contract with the government of Ethiopia to explore and develop natural energy resources in the Ogaden Basin.

Following an understanding between the two countries to establish a strategic partnership in 2017, China provided Djibouti with wide-ranging infrastructure assistance, among them highways and public buildings. Recognizing Djibouti's strategic location, and especially Ethiopia's dependency on Djibouti ports, the Chinese government also agreed to finance huge development projects, some of which have been jointly undertaken by Ethiopia and Djibouti and of which the Ogaden gas project was the single largest. The main projects include a $590 million Doraleh multipurpose port, a $3 billion overhaul and expansion of the original French colonial-era port, a $3.5 billion international free-trade zone, a $3.4 billion, 752.7-km Ethiopia-Djibouti railway, a $322 million Djibouti-Ethiopia water supply project and a $4 billion gas project, which consists of 767-900 km pipeline stretching from the gas fields of Ethiopia's Somali Region to a port in Djibouti and a gas treatment plant at the port. Other projects financed by China include two airports and fibre internet between Djibouti and Pakistan, which is then connected to mainland China.

Despite the huge Chinese investment in the Ogaden gas and oil project and other joint projects between Djibouti and Ethiopia, as well as the long-term agreements POLY-GCL had made with these two countries, Ethiopia did not stop talking to other potential investors in the Ogaden gas and oil project. Among the countries that have shown interest in the Ogaden gas project and that Ethiopia made deals with are the UAE and the USA. The UAE promised to finance a pipeline to transport the Ogaden gas through Eritrea instead of Djibouti, partly to avenge the latter for ending a contract with Dubai's DP World. DP World is one of the world's biggest port operators and used to run Djibouti's Doraleh container terminal.

The termination of the contract with Dubai's DP World in 2018 came after Djibouti made several cooperation agreements with China, of which the Ogaden gas and oil project is the most significant one. In response, the United Arab Emirates reached an agreement in 2018 with Ethiopia and Eritrea to build a pipeline from Addis Ababa to the Eritrean port of Assab to transport the Ogaden's gas and oil. The information regarding the building of the oil pipeline connecting Assab with Ethiopia was revealed in August 2018 during a meeting in Addis Ababa between the Ethiopian Prime Minister Abiy Ahmed and Reem Al Hashimy, the UAE's state minister for international cooperation.

In March 2022, Ethiopia signed a contract with a US company, Netherland, Sewell & Associates, Inc (NSAI), to investigate the extent of the oil and gas reserves in the Ogaden Basin. On 26 August 2022, the Ministry of Mines and Petroleum received from the company the first gas reserves certificate following the completion of a four-month study verifying the extent of the oil and natural gas reserves in Ethiopia and how to extract them. After he received the certificate, the Minister of Mines and Petroleum said 'This document is a confirmation certificate of Ethiopia's natural gas volume and economic viability. With this certificate, we can invite companies with technological, financial and investment potential at the international level. It also empowers the government's bargaining power'.[1] The minister's remarks and the ultimatum given to POLY-GCL indicated that Ethiopia was looking for other oil companies to take part in the scramble or replace POLY-GCL before the cancellation of POLY-GCL's contract.

So far, nothing practical has been done about the pipeline that the UAE promised to build, and that project is unlikely to materialise because of the political instability and the civil war in Ethiopia. For the same reasons, American companies are also unlikely to make huge investments in the Ogaden Basin for the time being. The fluid situation resulting from the political and security upheaval, as well as the real owners' absence from the management of their resources, puts the viability of the gas project in the Ogaden Basin in doubt, no matter whether it is run by the Chinese or by other would-be investors.

The current geopolitical infighting in the Horn also adversely impacts all ongoing economic activities in the country. The competition going on behind the scenes between the US and China is observable. The two countries nominated Horn of Africa envoys and sent them to the region. Additionally, China held a Horn conference attended by representatives from the Horn countries in Addis Ababa in June 2022.

The opposite views of the two powers in the Tigray war, which are reflected by the positions they took about the conflict in the Security Council of the United Nations, further indicate that geopolitical confrontation. Since the outbreak of the conflict, the US government has sympathised with Tigray and advocated for international intervention in the Security Council, whereas China, India and Russia did not criticise the government and rejected any intervention. It seems that Ethiopia is becoming a battleground for big powers such as China, India, Russia and Turkey on one side and the West on the other. All these countries have economic

---

[1] Addis Standard, News: Ethiopia's first certificate on gas reserves shows presence of seven trillion cubic feet in Ogaden Basin, August 26, 2022, https://addisstandard.com/news-ethiopias-first-certificate-on-gas-reserves-shows-presence-of-seven-trillion-cubic-feet-in-ogaden-basin/.

investments in Ethiopia, and each of them wants to have a say in the roadmap for the future development of that country.

Neither the outcome of the civil war nor the geopolitical infighting amongst the world powers is easy to predict. These correlated issues are interdependent in many ways. On the one hand, the winning side in the civil war will have the opportunity to decide which world power to align with. On the other hand, given the big fragmentation of the political actors and ethnic conflicts in the country, it is unlikely that an Ethiopian political force will gain control of the whole country without foreign intervention. The intervention of a single power is also doomed to fail because of likely counter-intervention from other world powers. This is an Ethiopian problem and, ideally, it should be up to the Ethiopians to put their house in order in the end, but Ethiopia's population does not agree even on the definition of nationhood. Besides that, there is not a political group with enough power to force a political programme.

That gloomy prediction for the political development in Ethiopia is a reflection of its artificial statehood and the contradictions of its political culture and behaviour. It is a country that consists of a union of nations forcibly brought together by the conquest of two ethnic groups and held together by military means. The two ethnic groups (Amhara and Tigray) that created Ethiopia are now tearing it apart, and the underdog ethnic groups that are the majority are unlikely to shed tears for the collapse of the state under which they have been suffering since their forced incorporation.

The Abyssinians (Tigray and Amhara) ruled the country since its formation through totalitarian systems of absolute monarchy followed by military regimes, except for the last five years. The current government came to power largely as the result of the Oromo and Amhara regions' uprising against the EPRDF regime, and these two nations dominate it. The current government system of ethnic federalism was introduced by the Tigray-led EPRDF regime that ruled Ethiopia in the period 1991-2018.

According to the proponent of the current federal system, the TPLF, the ethnic federal system was introduced primarily to address the nationhood issue by recognizing the fact that Ethiopia is not one nation as the preceding regimes claimed but a union of different nations lumped together involuntarily. 'Officially, the motive behind the introduction of the constitution was to recognise the multinational nature of the country and give the different nations self-rule over their regions within the republic, and even allow them to leave the union if they wished.'[1]

The introduction of the federal constitution was welcomed by most of the nations that make up the republic, but unfortunately the TPLF failed to implement the federal constitution on the ground. Instead, it selectively granted self-rule to Tigray and imposed central rule on others using deceptive tactics.

'The TPLF ruled the country directly and indirectly through the EPRDF umbrella organisation, which consisted of four parties from four regions (that is, Tigray, Amhara, Oromo and the Southern Nations). No other regions were allowed to join the ruling club, which the TPLF created and led. The four EPRDF regions were administrated by the EPRDF party, whereas the rest were led by TPLF-nominated administrations. Thus, the TPLF practically ruled the country using a two-tier system: through the EPRDF with other subordinate parties in the first tier and through the regional state administrations in the second tier. The federal system, which was supposed to devolve powers and establish administrations with different mandates at the federal, regional and district levels, became a one-party system in all levels of government.'[2]

In other words, it created a new type of totalitarian system guided by deception and enforced by military means and repression. That hypocrisy led to the war in the Ogaden, which lasted throughout the period of its rule, and the uprising in Oromo and Amhara regions that led to its downfall.

Despite the selective implementation of the constitution and the subsequent power misuse of the TPLF, most of the Ethiopian

---

[1] M M Abdi, *A history of the Ogaden (Western Somali) Struggle for Self Determination*, Part II (2007–2021), page 217.
[2] M M Abdi, *A history of the Ogaden (Western Somali) Struggle for Self Determination*, Part II (2007–2021), page 218.

people still think that ethnic federalism is the minimum devolution of power that can hold the country together. Recently, there have been fears about a return to the unitary system caused by the dominant position of the Amhara in government, the only ethnic group that favours the unitary system, but that fear is fading away due to the civil war. A disintegration or a looser union are the most likely outcomes of the conflict.

The current Tigray war is unlikely to cause dramatic changes in international relations or lead to military intervention by a world power despite the many world powers' political involvement in the conflict. However, an intervention by the tiny neighbouring country in the north, namely Eritrea, could have regional and beyond regional impacts. An intervention by Eritrea would probably lead to the defeat of the Tigray rebels and could avert the disintegration of Ethiopia in the short term if it is tolerated by external powers. But even such a military resolution cannot last long, and the current contentious political issues will remain unresolved in the long term. In addition to that, an Eritrean intervention would probably provoke a response from the West, which could reverse the outcome of the military resolution.

In short, any intervention, either regional or external, would have a minimal long-term effect because of the artificial nature of Ethiopian nationhood and the growing recognition of the inevitability of the disintegration of that unnatural empire by the nations that it consists of. Thus, implosion followed by separation of the nations is more likely than continued marriage. If Ethiopia survives, confederation is more likely than the current federal system.

Although the scramble for the natural resources of the Somali Region is a major component of the ongoing geopolitical infighting in the Horn, the Ogaden issue is not a game changer this time in the Horn conflict as it was during the 1970s. The 1977-78 Ogaden war changed the relations between West and East by ending détente, brought arms control talks to a halt and forced the superpowers to switch allegiance and support the conflicting sides.

However, the inhabitants of the Somali Region see the most

likely scenarios of disintegration or confederation as positive developments that can enhance their struggle for self-determination. The ongoing civil war has already halted the scramble for the Ogaden's natural resources, and genuine autonomy or separation from Ethiopia will enable the Somali people in the Ogaden to get back ownership of their land and natural resources.

4

The Remedy

4.1 Property Rights Restoration

Remediation for the scramble madness should start with the restoration of the property rights of the resources' real owners. Only when the rightful owners of the natural energy resources have unlimited property rights can they make the necessary planning for the feasibility study of the oil and gas project. Decisions on whether the natural resources are to be extracted or left untapped depend on whether the perceived economic benefits outweigh the economic, environmental and social costs. Finding out the best possible ways of extracting, developing, transporting and exporting the resources in the event of a decision to utilise them also needs proper investigation. A thorough and multidimensional examination is also required to test the viability and sustainability of the project to find out an optimal option for the utilisation of the natural resources.

Ownership restoration is not only an essential requirement for the conduct of a comprehensive feasibility study but is also vital for the sustainability of the project. Without the real owner's consent and without their full participation in all stages of the project, a peaceful environment conducive to carrying it out will not be attainable.

To see whether it is feasible, the focus must be on all the aspects of the project and their implications both in the short term and long term and not myopically concentrate on grabbing the resources, as has been the case so far. The project's direct and indirect consequences for the livelihoods of the inhabitants, the environment and the health of the population of the region must be part of the factors that determine the sustainability of the project.

As for the inhabitants of the land, whose livelihoods, health and dwelling places depend on the environmental suitability of the ground underneath which the geological resources lie, the exploitation activity affects their lives in many ways. Any damage to the environment affects their livelihoods and health. Adverse economic and social impacts caused by the forced removal of the inhabitants of the Ogaden Basin from their villages and the subsequent creation of the exclusion zones, such as loss of farming and grazing lands, have already hit the farmers and pastoralists directly.

Thus, because of the huge impacts the petroleum project has had on the daily lives of the inhabitants of the Basin and the fact that the resources belong to them, they know what is best for them. Accordingly, they can make appropriate decisions when undertaking the assessment of the feasibility, viability and sustainability of the project to ensure optimal utilisation of the natural gas and oil. Full ownership of the project by the indigenous people will therefore lead to a proper feasibility study, a sustainable project plan and thereby an optimal utilisation of the geological resources.

An enterprise run by the inhabitants of the land and the owners of its natural resources is expected to lead to the enhancement of the protection of the environment and redress its adverse impacts on social, health and economic issues. Proper use of labour and capital and the consequent increase in productivity, as well as optimal utilisation of the natural resources, are also more likely if the legitimate stakeholders run the business of the gas and oil project.

4.2 Feasibility and Viability Studies

The next step after the restoration of the ownership is to examine the feasibility of the project. Despite the long exploration history of the natural energy resources in the Ogaden Basin, comprehensive feasibility and viability studies based on cost/benefit analyses have not been conducted by the Ethiopian state and its scramble partners, or by the inhabitants of the region.

The reason for the lack of such studies is the illicit way the project started and the absence of the sole legitimate owners of the natural resources. The scramble alliance wanted to grab as much as possible of the natural resources at the expense of the owners. In their assessment of the profitability of the project, the exploiters only estimated the quantity and the value of the reserves of the natural resources, and the cost associated with the production (exploration, extraction, development and transportation) of the gas and oil. The share ratio of investment and production revenue between the government and the foreign oil companies were based on these costs and the expected revenue of the production. Thus, other aspects of the project, such as social net benefit and other costs, were not taken into consideration.

To ameliorate the unsustainable situation of the project, first, the business plan should start with a feasibility study to test the workability of the project, which is to see whether the fundamental conditions for carrying out such a project are fulfilled from a business point of view. The input factors (labour capital) and other related variables, such as technological capacity, the market and the suitability of the legal framework to the business, will be the main determining parameters of the feasibility of the project. After having verified the profitability of the business using these variables, and thereby its feasibility, the next step will be to check the viability of the business.

The viability of the project is determined by key factors that include the market, the finance, the technical know-how, the management and the business model. In addition to its business profitability, the project plan should take into consideration all the other factors that affect the survival of the project in one way or the other.

Specifically, the viability assessment involves the identification and estimation of the costs and the revenue of the production, as well as external costs in the long term. For a business to be viable, it must have the ability to survive, adaptability to change and the ability to ensure the long-term profitability of the business.

4.3 Sustainable Project Plan

Sustainability is defined by the UN's Brundtland Commission in 1987 as 'meeting the needs of the present without compromising the ability of future generations to meet their own needs'.[1] The concept is broken into three pillars: economic, environmental and social. These three components are informally referred to as profits, planet and people.

According to that definition, a sustainable project plan should take into consideration the feasibility and viability as well as the environmental, social, economic and health consequences of the project for both the present and future generations. In other words, these factors should be the main elements that form the basis of the business model.

Feasibility and viability are preconditions for sustainability; however, they are not the only factors that determine the sustainability of a business. In general terms, the sustainability of a business can be obtained when its financial, social and environmental risks are successfully managed. In addition to these three aspects, political and legal conditions conducive to business development are required for the sustainability of any project. In other words, all the crucial factors for sustainability must be integrated and included in the business model.

To check the sustainability of the project, it is required to examine first and foremost whether the expected benefits of the utilisation of the now available natural energy resources, namely the gas and oil, outweigh all the production-related costs, as well as the negative environmental, health, social and economic impacts of the project. The examination of the adaptability of the fossil fuel project to external pressures, such as climate change, is also required. The central issue here is to investigate whether the expected benefits of the utilisation of the available geological resources outweigh both the production and external costs, and accordingly decide on

---

[1] The UN, the United Nations Brundtland Commission 1987, Academic impact, page 1, https://www.un.org/en/academic-impact/sustainability.

whether to extract the oil and gas at all or leave it underneath the earth.

Considering the environmental pressures caused by climate change and the increasing demand by the entire world to replace high-carbon economies with low-carbon ones, a reassessment of the profitability of the project from an environmental point of view is paramount. Due to the growing global awareness of environmental problems, new environmental protection commitments are made by the nations of the world and are gradually coming into force. The global drive to move from fossil-fuel-intensive energy sources to low- or zero-carbon energy sources and the increasing switch from fossil-fuelled to electricity-fuelled vehicles indicate that the golden age of fossil fuels is gone. By the time the Ogaden gas and oil reaches the world markets, their value will be lower than today, and this is expected to dwindle further on a permanent basis due to the new drive to use renewables as a substitute for high-carbon energy sources.

A sustainable project plan also requires continuous evaluation of all the aspects of the project, which include its profitability and its adaptability to unpredictable changes from a business point of view, its impacts on social, environmental and equitable sharing and above all the acceptability of the legal political framework under which the project is to be carried out. The continuous fulfilment of these conditions is a requirement for the long-term sustainability of the plan.

The gas and oil project in the Ogaden Basin does not fulfil the conditions for viability and sustainability because it lacks key determining factors. The project started without proper planning in a hostile environment, and it is still going on in the way it began. Persistent security problems caused by the illicit method of grabbing the land and its natural energy resources prevented proper planning and effective execution of the project.

The occupation process was still in progress when the scramble began without a business plan. It started with a limited exploration aimed at detecting the presence of oil and natural gas in places where signs of oil seeps were seen. Because of the occupation and the ensuing scramble for the natural resources of the region, the Ogaden Basin has become a conflict zone, and as a result, the fossil fuel project there has been in turmoil since it was launched by the occupant and its associates in the illicit exploitation.

Despite the long period of forced incorporation, the political status of the Somali Region is unsettled, as indicated by the long struggle of the inhabitants for independence. The freedom dream is prevalent despite the current respite in the armed struggle, and the Ethiopian state has not shown any shift in its policy towards the occupation.

Due to the rigid positions of the two parties to the conflict on the status issue, a resolution to the conflict does not seem to be forthcoming soon. The conflict over the self-determination issue and the subsequent insecurity, repression and human rights violations are the main impediments to a sustainable project plan.

The scramble project itself fuelled the conflict. The quest for fossil fuels in the region was the main cause of the conquest, and throughout the period of the exploitation, the project was run by an alliance consisting of the Ethiopian state and foreign companies backed by its successive governments. With regard to the establishment and the running of the oil and gas project, the inhabitants have been ignored, as their wishes were not respected when their land was conquered by the same alliance. The position of the indigenous people regarding the scramble for their natural resources hardened with the intensification and internationalisation of the illicit exploitation and the consequent adverse environmental, health and livelihood impacts of the project that already affected them.

Although the federal parliament passed a general law on the profit sharing of natural resources, which for the first time stated a formula for sharing the profit from the natural resources, practically nothing new has happened on the ground. The inhabitants of the region are still absent from the project and are not taking part in any of its stages. Additionally, no new assessment was made on the project, and everything is going according to the plan of the scramble alliance.

Because of the unresolved political, legal and security issues, an environment conducive to business development is not achievable in the Somali Region. The lack of the existence of a business-friendly environment is an impediment to sustainable project planning.

Given these political, legal and security problems, the establishment of a project of this magnitude in the Somali Region will not be feasible, let alone viable or sustainable. Thus, the logical thing is to resolve these contentious issues before undertaking a project of this type.

4.4 Optimal Use of the Geological Resources

Optimal use of the geological resources currently under exploration (gas and oil) is predicated here by the sustainability of their business model. In other words, we use sustainability as the indicator of optimal use. In assessing the sustainability of the project, both short- and long-term production, social and environmental costs of the gas and oil project and its expected revenue are to be compared to reach an optimal decision. In short, only when the expected revenue is more than all the expected costs can the utilisation of the resources be optimal, and the extraction of the resources be a better option than leaving them untapped.

As mentioned in the previous section, the project is neither viable nor sustainable in its present form due to the current impediments. In the future, other expected challenges will further adversely affect it. To make the project sustainable and at the same time maintain that desired condition, it must satisfy the requirements of all business aspects needed for the attainment of that goal. Furthermore, to ensure the optimal use of the natural energy resources, the obstacles hindering the sustainability of the project must be addressed, and their remedy should be included in the business model of the project.

The logical conclusion from this is to find out the causes of the impediments and find out how to overcome them to achieve the goal of sustainability, and afterwards consider how to keep that desired level. In the following section, we will outline the main obstacles that are hampering the sustainability of the project now or that will affect it in the long term, and how to deal with these obstacles.

4.4.1 Current Optimisation Impediments

The parameters that adversely affect the sustainability of the project consist of current and future obstacles, which also impact one another. The current impediments are caused by government policies, whereas future challenges would be driven mainly by climate change and intergenerational wealth-sharing issues. Security, environmental, health and social issues are the main factors that influence the sustainability of the fossil fuels project both in the short term and the long term, whereas the intergenerational equity issue affects it in the long term.

The security problem that resulted from the occupation of the region, the scramble for its natural resources, the ensuing repression and the consequent resistance by the inhabitants of the region is the main obstacle currently hampering proper project planning and the optimal use of the fossil energy resources in the Somali Region. Due to the persistent insecurity, the utilisation of the resources has not been possible.

The insecurity is exacerbated by repressive policies related to the scramble, which included a general crackdown, gross human rights violations, the displacement of people, the destruction of property, the disruption of livelihoods, environmental damage and the outbreak of unknown diseases allegedly caused by chemical spills. These negative scramble impacts on the region have been detailed in chapter 2 and therefore there is no need to repeat them here.

The brutal way the project is currently run by the Ethiopian government and its scramble partners will also adversely affect the project in the long term by worsening the security problem and by leading to further delays in the utilisation of the energy resources. Due to the security problems caused by the occupation and the scramble and the subsequent exclusion of the owners of the resources from the exploitation project, it has not been possible to utilise the natural energy resources up to now, and because of the delay and the global drive to increase the use of renewable energy, the resources are losing their value.

As a result of the persistent security problem, the Ogaden Basin fossil fuels are unlikely to reach the world markets for decades to come, despite the relentless efforts by the scramble alliance to utilise them soon. Any longer delay will further reduce the value of the resources and will therefore undermine the viability and sustainability of the project. Additionally, environmental pressures caused by climate change are expected to lead to a reduction in the demand for fossil fuels and an increase in the use of renewables.

4.4.2 Future Optimisation Challenges

Given the huge proven gas reserves of the Ogaden Basin and the high world demand for gas for the time being, and excluding all other factors, the Basin's gas project seems profitable; however, it might not be so many years to come because of the environmental pressures to reduce the dependency on fossil fuels in the short and medium terms and phase them out completely in the long term. Delays caused by conflicts and the illicit exploitation have already reduced the value of the reserves, and that adverse effect will continue if the deferment of utilisation and its root causes remain unresolved. In addition to that, the usefulness of the project might be questioned due to intergenerational justice considerations.

In this section, we will briefly examine these external pressures and how to deal with their impacts on fossil fuel energy. Specifically, the global efforts to replace fossil fuels with renewable energy and their implications for the fossil fuels of the Somali Region will be examined. The implications of the issue of equitable sharing between the current and future generations will also be discussed.

Due to climate change, which is caused by human activity and driven largely by increased carbon dioxide emissions into the atmosphere, pressure to reduce and even abandon carbon-intensive fuels is growing. The impact of climate change is widespread and affects the whole globe. Both the rich and the poor parts of the world are affected by them, though the poorest bear the brunt of the impact.

Greenhouse gas emissions from fossil fuels are the dominant cause of climate change. Solar energy reflected by the Earth's surface is radiated back into the atmosphere as heat. As the heat makes its way through the atmosphere and back out to space, greenhouse gases released into the atmosphere by the burning of coal, gas and oil absorb much of it. They then radiate some of the heat back to the Earth's surface, and most of the current climate change is attributed to very small variations in Earth's orbit that change the amount of solar energy our planet receives. Increased levels of greenhouse gases cause the Earth to warm up in response and thereby increase the temperature of the Earth's surface. The rise in the temperature in turn leads to climate change, which includes declining mountain glaciers, the acceleration of ice melting in cold places, rising sea levels, flooding, recurrent droughts and desertification.

Because of the universal nature of climate change, there is a global realisation of the seriousness of the environmental challenges it poses and the necessity to tackle it. As indicated by international climate agreements such as the 1992 United Nations Framework Convention on Climate Change (UNFCCC), the 1997 Kyoto Protocol, the 2015 UN Climate Change Conference (COP21) in Paris and the 2021 UN Climate Change Conference (COP26) in Glasgow, the nations of the world have made commitments to reduce global warming.

The UNFCCC established the first international environmental treaty to combat dangerous human interference with the climate. At the UNFCCC, the signatories pledged to reduce greenhouse gas emissions, based on the scientific consensus.

The countries that ratified the Kyoto Protocol agreed to implement the objective of the UNFCCC to reduce the onset of global warming by reducing greenhouse gas concentrations in the atmosphere to a level that would not pose dangers to the climate. However, the obligation to reduce emissions was placed on developed countries because of the recognition that they were historically responsible for the current levels of emissions in the atmosphere.

At the UN Climate Change Conference (COP21) in Paris, the participants collectively agreed to keep global warming well under 2 degrees Celsius through mitigation. Although developing countries were encouraged to contribute voluntarily to the efforts, developed nations agreed again in Paris to take the lead in reducing emissions and also pledged to provide financial support to poor nations that were vulnerable to climate challenges to deal with difficulties brought by climate change.

The 2021 UN Climate Change Conference (COP26) in Glasgow further strengthened the commitments made in the previous agreements. More climate finance for developing countries to adapt to climate change was promised in Glasgow. Further, the participants agreed to greater emission reductions, and they explicitly committed for the first time to reduce the use of coal. Efforts to change these commitments into reality by the international community are on the way.

Due to the environmental pressures and the consequent urgency to address them, the future of fossil fuel energy hangs in the balance. Environmentally friendly energy sources are now prioritised by the international community. Renewable energy sources are now attractive and are hugely invested in by both the public and the private sectors. The investment primarily consists of research into energy transition and the creation of structures for renewables.

The transportation industry seems to have taken the lead in the energy transition by replacing petrol- and diesel-driven engines with electric ones. In recent years, private cars and public transport fuelled by electricity have increased, and more vehicles are expected to be fuelled by electricity.

Huge global efforts are underway to make available renewable energy sources that could replace high-carbon energy sources.

Power generation based on renewables with zero or minimal greenhouse gas emissions is the focus now. Of the many renewables in use (hydro energy, solar energy, wind energy, tidal energy, geothermal energy and biomass energy), the first three are the most heavily invested in and the most widely used. In many parts of the world, hydroelectric power, wind power and solar power generate a large amount of electricity. However, because of their technological advantages, industrialised nations are the primary producers and users of these renewable energy resources.

Hydroelectric power, wind power and solar power are the main renewable energy sources that generate electricity. They are also the main energy sources replacing fossil fuels in the energy transformation from high-carbon energy to clean energy. According to International Renewable Energy Agency (IRENA), more than 80 percent of all electricity capacity added last year was renewables, with solar and wind accounting for more than 90 percent of the renewables. As the following brief summary of these three renewables indicates, they are gradually replacing fossil fuels in many parts of the world and are expected to have an impact on the fossil fuels in the Somali Region.

Hydroelectric power is a form of renewable energy generated by the movement of water. Water has been used by mankind for thousands of years to power machines that were used mainly for irrigation and other labour-intensive tasks. In 1831, the first electric generator was invented by Michael Faraday, and with that invention, the utilisation of hydroelectric power began. Following that discovery, small-scale hydroelectric power plants were set up. Due to technological advances, these plants gradually grew both in number and size.

Hydroelectric power plants are located on rivers, streams, and canals; but for reliable and sustainable energy generation, water storage behind dams is necessary. All types of hydroelectric facilities are powered by the kinetic energy of flowing water as it moves downstream. Turbines and generators are used to convert that kinetic energy into electricity, which is then fed into the electrical grid, from which the users get the electricity they need.

Currently, hydroelectric power produces 16 percent of global electricity and is the largest renewable generating electricity. The potential of hydroelectric power capacity is expected to increase further because of the push for more green energy, though the percentage increase is anticipated to be less than that of solar and wind power.

Ethiopia is to become a major producer of hydroelectric power. Currently, Ethiopia's electricity is mainly generated by hydroelectric power, and when the Grand Ethiopian Renaissance Dam (GERD) project, which is the largest in Africa, is completed, it will become a big hydroelectric nation and an exporter of hydroelectric power.

Wind power is the second most widely used renewable energy source. It has been used for thousands of years for a variety of purposes, which include sport, food production, sailing and power generation. The two biggest usages of wind energy are power generation and popular sports. Sailing, kitesurfing and kiteboarding are some of the sports that rely on wind energy. The new interest shown by shipping companies in embracing wind energy to reduce fuel costs and their carbon footprint further expanded the demand of wind energy.

However, wind energy's biggest usage has been power generation. To harness electricity from wind energy, turbines are used to drive generators connected to them. The turbines have huge blades mounted on tall towers. As the wind starts to move the blades of the turbines the generators start to turn, which then produce electricity. Several wind turbines may be grouped together and connected to the electric power transmission network to establish a wind farm.

The first electricity-generating turbine was created in 1887 by a Scottish academic, James Blyth. He built the world's first wind turbine to provide electricity for the lighting of his holiday home. Wind power usage has increased recently as a response to the high demand for renewables caused by climate change. According to the International Renewable Energy Agency (IRENA), the production of electricity from wind power doubled between 2009 and 2013 and is increasing. Wind energy accounts for about 5 percent of global electricity.

Solar power is the third most important source of renewable energy, after wind and hydroelectric energy. Solar power is the conversion of energy from sunlight into electricity. Solar energy, which is the heat and radiant light from the sun, is harnessed using modern technology such as photovoltaics, which converts sunlight directly into electricity, or concentrated solar power, which converts it indirectly, or a combination.

According to historians, humans began lighting fires by concentrating the sun's light through a magnifying glass from as early as the seventh century B.C., and the first solar oven was invented in 1767. This mechanism of utilizing sunlight to heat meals or drinks is still prevalent today in areas of the world that do not have access to electricity. Alexander Edmond Becquerel, a French physicist, discovered the photovoltaic (PV) effect in 1839 and the discovery of the PV effect laid the groundwork for solar technology to come. Huge technological advances have been made since then, and solar energy use has widened both in scope and quantity. Solar panels are used today to power, among other things homes, businesses and satellites.

Solar power accounts for over 3 percent of global electricity generation and about 6 percent of electricity generated by renewables. The solar energy share of renewables has been increasing in recent years, and the solar PV segment contributes most of that growth. The Asia Pacific region is the largest market for solar PV energy, and China is leading the world in solar PV production. The US and the European Union are ranked second and third, respectively, in the share market for solar energy.

Climate change and the consequent shift of energy sources from fossil fuels to renewables will impact the Ogaden Basin project directly and indirectly and put the long-term sustainability of the economically feasible project into question. Through the likely long-term reduction of demand for fossil fuels and the expected extra costs associated with the necessary adjustment for environmental challenges, climate change affects the project. The environmental challenges, the intergenerational equity issue and the illicit exploitation all need to be reviewed before undertaking the project.

The sustainability of the existing oil and gas project in the Ogaden Basin depends on both historical obstacles and future challenges. In other words, solving the political and legal disputes that have hampered its utilisation so far, tackling the equitable sharing issue and the project's adaptability to the environmental challenges will be crucial to the sustainability of the project.

From the intergenerational justice perspective, the environmental element also takes centre stage. The generations that utilise the geological resources may get economic compensation for the environmental damage caused by the exploration and production operations, but the generations that will come after the fossil fuels have dried up or lost value share the environmental damage with previous generations but will not get the economic benefits from the resources, unless the present generation puts aside a portion of the income for coming generations.

Ideally, equitable wealth and burden sharing between the current and future generations should be part of the business model of the fossil fuels project. Responsibility for this obligation falls on the current generation because the planning and the establishment of the project are initiated by it. Unfortunately, the current generation of indigenous inhabitants of the region has been excluded from the project. Since the current generation is voiceless, talk of intergenerational justice is not relevant here.

The scramble for the natural energy resources of the Somali Region started at the beginning of the petroleum industry boom. However, the project is still in the exploration stage and, as mentioned earlier, the international community is making serious effort to reduce or get rid of entirely the use of fossil fuels. Besides that, the security problems that delayed its utilisation and their root causes are still unresolved. These external impediments put the viability and sustainability of the otherwise profitable project in doubt.

The long-term sustainability of the fossil fuel project depends on the continuous viability of the fundamental facets of the business and its capability to handle internal and external challenges.

Continuous evaluation of these elements is necessary to ensure the continuation of sustainability. Additionally, the project should be adaptable to unpredictable changes.

4.4.3 Tackling the Optimisation Challenges

The conflict, the illicit exploitation, the consequent exclusion of the owners from the project and the lack of compensation for health damage, environmental impacts and livelihood disruption are currently the main hindrance to sustainability. In addition to these related problems, environmental challenges resulting from climate change will affect the project in the future and for that reason, the project is required to be adaptable to deal with these international challenges. The future sustainability of the project depends on both the historical impediments currently affecting it and the impeding climate-related challenges mentioned above, but so far, these obstacles have not been taken into consideration by the scramble alliance.

The root causes of the current main bottlenecks to sustainability are contentious political issues relating to the issue of self-determination and the scramble for the resources of the region, and these issues have been dealt with in chapter 2 and section 4.4.2. In this section, we will concentrate on the environmental challenges emanating from climate change. The effects of these challenges on the future sustainability and adaptability of the project to these external pressures will be outlined.

If the oil and gas from the Ogaden Basin ever reach the world market, they will certainly be affected by the environmental pressures caused by climate change. A timely response to the frequently changing demand patterns for energy sources and innovations to meet environmental challenges are the two main elements of the adaptability that the project must have.

The negative effects of climate change and increasing global awareness of the environmental challenges caused by greenhouse gases have given new impetus to the decarbonisation drive. Consequently, the international community has decided to replace fossil fuels with renewables in the long term, and steps towards that endeavour have already been taken. Many countries and companies have already made pledges to become carbon neutral by 2050 and are increasingly investing in renewables to achieve that goal. As a result of the decarbonisation push, both supply and demand for fossil fuels are set to decline. However, though the replacement processes are in progress, it will take time to achieve the goal of carbon neutralisation.

The seemingly inevitable decarbonisation of energy has two main imperatives for the oil and gas industry: to sell as much as possible of the fossil fuels while there is demand for them and to make the necessary energy transition adjustments to meet the environmental requirements of the future. In other words, the available products must be used before they expire, and life extension measures should be devised for those that can survive the challenges.

Fossil fuels seem indispensable in the short term as there are no other available energy sources that can fully replace them. Gas, and especially liquefied natural gas (LNG), is expected to have relative longevity and survive during the transition period and beyond because of its relatively low carbon footprint compared to coal and oil and because of the possibility of modifying it and using it in combination with renewables in a hybrid system. But in the long run, even LNG will ultimately be replaced by renewable energy sources unless it undergoes emissions mitigation to meet future environmental requirements.

The demand for the environmental modifications of fossil fuels is growing, and some product adjustments are already in the pipeline. Using carbon capture, utilisation and storage (CCUS) technology, carbon neutralisation processes of LNG plants are ongoing in many parts of the world.

In accordance with that trend, the Ogaden Basin project must have strategies to deal with the impending challenges: specifically, it must prepare for the inevitable reduction in the demand for fossil fuels and sell as much as possible of the products while they are still in use. In addition to that, it must adapt modern technologies and make the necessary product adjustments to decarbonise and meet the ever-hardening environmental requirements when fossil fuels are no longer in demand in their original form. Besides that, it must have an inbuilt learning capacity to continuously modify or develop alternative products to stay in the energy business.

Although some oil was found in the Ogaden, the amount of oil has not been verified. However, natural gas is available in large quantities and is expected to last many decades to come. For that reason, our focus is on the adaptability of the gas industry to environmental pressures.

The Ukraine war has led to energy supply shortages and consequently to high energy prices. However, both the demand for and the price of gas were increasing prior to the Russian invasion of Ukraine. The demand for gas has skyrocketed recently, and that high demand is expected to continue at least into the next decade, with seasonal adjustments. The recent surge in demand prior to the Ukraine war, is partly due to supply shortages allegedly caused by delays over the approval of a newly built gas pipeline between Russia and Europe, which is now terminated due to the ongoing Ukraine war, and partly by long-term factors.

Russia was accused of holding back supplies to speed up approval of the newly built Nord Stream 2 pipeline running directly from Russia to Germany. It was alleged that the Russian gas company Gazprom intentionally withheld supplies to force the German regulator and the European Commission to approve the pipeline. Russia denied the accusation and declared that it met its contractual obligations. It claimed that there were spot demands that it could not deliver. Whatever the cause, the discrepancy between the demand and the supply of Russian gas has had an immediate effect on both the global demand and the price of gas. The big Asian markets have also contributed to the recent surge in gas demand and the consequent price rises, but most of the high demand from the Asian markets are caused by long-term factors related to industrial changes.

Two important developments led to the surge in demand for gas in Asian markets: a rapid increase in power-sector demand, followed by a sizeable increase in the switch of energy sources from coal to gas by key energy-intensive industries, such as the chemical industry. Natural gas is relatively clean compared to both oil and coal, and in addition to that, gas is increasingly used in combination with renewables. Additionally, gas and renewable energy sources can be scaled at speed and require complementary technologies. As an example, onshore- and offshore-wind generation and solar PV are intermittent and are often backed up by gas plants to power the grid in low-wind or cloudy conditions.

Despite the recent price surge of gas, on average its price was falling in key markets before the Ukraine invasion, especially in North America, and price reduction in the long term is likely. Because of the lower price of gas relative to other fossil fuels and the fact that gas has a lower carbon footprint than other fossil fuels per unit of energy, the demand for natural gas is likely to grow, at least in the energy transition period. The increasing substitution of coal by gas not only reinforces the current high demand for gas, but also demonstrates the importance of natural gas, especially LNG, in the transitional period. LNG will probably be the last fossil fuel to be replaced.

Not only the future is uncertain for fossil fuel energy because of the drive to phase them out, but also because of the lack of standardised system of environmental requirements in the energy transition. The gas industry is expected to be instrumental in the energy transition; however, the industry's longevity depends on its ability to reduce emissions. But despite general guidelines making emission mitigation the determining parameter of the future use of gas, there are no specific international standards on emission level requirements. Therefore, the industry must prepare for the energy transition with these uncertainties.

Despite these uncertainties, the industry knows that decarbonisation is what is required, and in making the preparation for the transition and beyond, the industry must take a number of steps in advance to meet the anticipated challenges. The main awaited challenge is the obligation to mitigate emissions, and the first issue that the companies in the gas industry must concentrate on to make that preparation is information gathering regarding emissions. Specifically, the asset's emissions over time, its emission cost and its modification potential are the main factors that must be taken into consideration in the business plan.

Gas companies need to develop emission categorisation systems to record emissions and monitor them at every step of the value chain, and differentiation among various greenhouse gases should be included in the emission reporting system. The record of the asset's emissions over its life cycle is vital for its evaluation because that information will be used by the authorities and end users in deciding its future use.

The emission costs will be paid by the polluter in the end, either in the form of tax or price reductions, and hence the gas industry should integrate emission risks and costs into the business model after having accepted responsibility for the emissions and recorded them. In other words, the companies investing in the gas business must incorporate costs associated with emissions into their calculations of returns on investment to get an accurate picture of the viability of gas projects.

Decarbonisation should also be part of the long-term survival strategy of the gas industry and hence should be part of the business model. Given the expected extra costs caused by emission reduction requirements, new project investments should aim to reduce production costs by either reducing emissions of the existing products using CCUS technology or by investing in renewables, and the project plan should include both measures.

The uncertainties related to the decarbonisation drive and emission risks that are expected to hamper the sustainability of the gas industry will have ramifications for the Ogaden Basin project. Additionally, the project's sustainability was already in limbo due to the security problems, the lack of sustainable business plan and so on. Thus, the survival of the Ogaden Basin gas industry depends on solving both its historical problems and the future challenges caused by decarbonisation pledges, which it shares with the rest of the industry.

The historical obstacles to the sustainability of the project and how to overcome them were outlined in the previous sections, and for that reason we will merely mention here the impediments related to the energy transition period. In addition to the uncertainties outlined above concerning the whole gas industry, which originated from climate change and the consequent new environmental requirements, the Ogaden Basin project lacks transparency. This problem will hinder future planning and thereby any progress toward decarbonisation and adaptability unless it is resolved.

Transparency is key to the survival of the industry because emissions must be recorded and categorised, and greenhouse gases should be differentiated. The products must be labelled so that the emission information is communicable to the customers and the regulators. The project must have internal transparency too, to examine its future sustainability and consider the extra costs associated with the reduction of emissions and possible product modifications.

For the time being, the gas project in the Somali Region is not run by the indigenous people. The Ethiopian government and foreign companies are responsible for the management of the project and the primary stakeholders, namely the inhabitants of the region, are excluded from all its stages. From this, it is clear that talk of transparency, either internal or external, is out of the question, and without transparency, it will not be possible to make a sustainable business plan or to make preparations for the energy transition.

5

Lessons from Other Countries

5.1 Norway's Oil and Gas Industry: A Success Model

The Norwegian petroleum industry has a fascinating history. It is not only a success story, but a unique model. The country developed a management framework with a long-term perspective designed to maximise the utilisation of gas and oil, while at the same time minimizing the damage to the environment and other natural resources. In other words, it is a sustainable business model that aims to optimise the use of resources and ensure equitable distribution of income from natural resources between present and future generations.

The success of the model is predicated on the pillars of sustainability (namely optimal utilisation of resources), environmental protection, technological innovation, adaptability and intergenerational justice. In other words, the model's positive impacts on these important issues are what made the Norwegian experiment a success story. The focus of the examination here is what led to the positive outcome of the model.

The success of the model was the result of a concerted effort by the state and the private sector. The state laid down a business framework for the petroleum industry, which it directed, but the private sector played a key role in its implementation.

The Norwegian offshore oil experiment began with the demarcation of its continental shelf and the declaration of state ownership of the shelf and its resources. An American oil company called Philips found oil on the Netherlands shelf of the North Sea, and because of that discovery, the company suspected the presence of oil on the Norwegian shelf and informed the Norwegian authorities of its desire to explore. But when Phillips sought oil exploration concessions on the Norwegian shelf in 1962, Norway refused to grant exploration rights until its maritime borders were cleared with its neighbours.

After having secured sovereign rights over an offshore area several times larger than its mainland and declared state ownership of its continental shelf, it began the concession process in 1965. In that year, 22 production licences covering a total of 78 blocks were awarded to oil companies. The first discovery of oil was made in 1969. The Ekofisk field, where the first discovery happened, started production in 1971.

The development of a business framework directed by the state but jointly carried out by the private and public sectors was the next step. Norway did not have the technological capability to extract gas and oil from beneath the sea, and for that reason it relied on other nations, especially the US, to conduct the deep offshore oil operations there. Philips, the US company that triggered the oil exploration there, took the lead. The foreign companies were responsible for the exploration and development of gas and oil fields in the initial stages. However, both the Norwegian government and leading local companies systematically planned to acquire the necessary expertise to get full control over the management of their resources in the long term. Through a combination of local technological innovation and technological transfer measures, Norway gradually began the Norwegianisation of the oil and gas industry.

The determination to Norwegianise the industry led to the establishment of a service and supply industry for petroleum. The service and supply industry for the petroleum sector, which was started by leading private industrialists, grew rapidly. The industry is now the second largest industry (after the sale of oil and gas). It also extended its services and supplies to other industries, such as the wind energy industry, and it is a competent and competitive industry in both local and global markets.

The government and the sectors of maritime and energy were

the driving forces behind the indigenisation push. The government introduced policies encouraging the local industry to take over as much as possible of the oil and gas operations, and these sectors provided the practical tools to achieve the indigenisation goal.

Before the oil discovery, Norway had a large shipping industry and was a big hydroelectric power-producing nation. Using their expertise in shipbuilding and the construction of hydroelectric dams, leading Norwegian companies enthusiastically entered the race for the hunt of oil and gas soon after the discovery of oil. These companies were able to quickly convert the skills they had from the shipping and energy sectors to the maritime side of offshore oil activities.

The Norwegian shipping companies began their work regarding offshore oil activities with the construction of semisubmersible drilling rigs. The repair of a damaged American rig that was done in Norway by a local company (Aker) opened the door for contracts in the oil and gas sector. After they demonstrated their ability to use their maritime skills for the repair of that rig, they established themselves within a short period in the oil and gas sector and got contracts for the construction of rigs from both foreign oil companies and the domestic service and supply industry. The construction of semisubmersible drilling rigs became a booming business afterwards and also became a large part of the service and supply industry.

The Norwegian companies had the ambition to supply rigs not only to the Norwegian market but also to the international markets, and they had rapid success in that endeavour. The international-oriented Norwegian companies soon made cooperation understandings with several European shipyards to create rigs, and one of the leading Norwegian companies, namely the Aker Group, developed its own semisubmersible (Aker H3) in 1974. The creation of H3 and their wide network in the European shipyards enabled the Norwegian ship-owners to dominate the rig market on the North Sea continental shelves within a short period.

The other industry that contributed to the growth of the service and supply industry for petroleum was hydroelectric power. Philips, the American oil company responsible for the operation of the Ekofisk field, decided to keep its early production in a large storage tank, and the offshore platforms needed legs to stand on, both of which were decided to be built from concrete. Inspired by the concrete-made tank, the Norwegian contractors soon developed concepts for platform legs using their skills for the construction of hydroelectric dams.

After building the store tank, Norwegian contractors began building offshore platforms using concrete for the platforms' legs. The building work of the first platform began in June 1973, when the group made a deal with the Mobil oil company for the construction of a concrete platform structure for the 118-meter-deep Beryl field on the British continental shelf. The structure for Beryl A was successfully completed and installed in 1975. Before they finished that first project, the group got contracts from the domestic market as well. As their first project that was carried out outside Norway indicated, their platform technology became a global brand.

Due to the innovation of the service and supply industry, the government's push for the advancement of local technology and the inflow into Norway of foreign operators seeking to solve offshore technological challenges there, the Norwegian continental shelf became a laboratory for developing new technology. Consequently, Norway has not only gained a technological edge in petroleum operations, but it has also become a global testing ground for new technologies relating to offshore petroleum operations and renewable energy.

In addition to that remarkable contribution by the service and supply industry, the government planned and worked systematically to obtain local know-how with the capacity to carry out the operations of the oil and gas sector. Because of their technological advantages and the need to learn from them, foreign oil companies were given financial incentives, which included tax reductions and lower royalties, to commit themselves to the continental shelf of Norway. However, the government did not want to depend on their expertise in the long term, and therefore it contemplated ways of reducing their dominance and strived to gain the required knowledge to run the industry themselves.

As the oil industry was growing, so was the Norwegian government becoming more determined to get full control of all the aspects of the gas and oil operations. The process of reducing their dependency on foreign companies began in earnest about a year after the first production of oil, with implementable steps.

Through a combination of technological transfer and innovation, Norway strived to gain technological capabilities that could enable it to take over the operations of the oil and gas fields. To achieve that goal, the government did two things. First, it introduced regulations aimed to boost technological transfer and increase local involvement in offshore activities. Second, it created a company, Statoil (Equinor), to administer the oil and gas resources.

The principle of 50 percent state participation in each production licence was introduced. Concession arrangements were not only made dependent on Norwegian participation in all stages, but foreign companies seeking allocation were also required to do at least 50 percent of the research and training related to the development of fields to operate in Norway. Additionally, the local industries were encouraged to increase their involvement in offshore operations and, consequently, Norwegian skill was to be developed within all technological sectors of the oil and gas industry.

For foreign companies, Norwegianisation implied both restrictions and rewards since contracts and other benefits were tied to their contribution to the indigenisation efforts. Foreign oil companies contributed to the Norwegianisation efforts after they realised that they would not be given contracts without their contribution, and the stick and carrot measures that the authorities used to ensure the eventual indigenisation of the industry were effective, especially after they became part of the daily routine.

However, when Norway achieved the indigenisation of the operation of its oil and gas industry, it reversed its protectionist policies. The protectionist regulations that Norway employed mainly to gain technological transfer were relaxed after Statoil and other Norwegian companies involved in the petroleum business become competent international actors. Due to the indigenisation efforts, Norway today exports the products and the technology it used to import when the oil business began there.

The practical processes of the indigenisation operation officially began with the formation of a state-owned oil company and the introduction of new regulations intended to speed up the transfer of technology, and the new oil company was given the responsibility to coordinate the Norwegianisation processes. In 1972, Statoil was established to manage the oil and gas resources of Norway. The state-owned oil company has successfully managed these resources since then, and it became a global company conducting oil and gas operations in many parts of the world. The company was partly privatised, but the state still owns over 60 percent of its shares. In 2018, the company changed its name to Equinor.

Statoil was established primarily to become an operator running all the stages of the oil operation processes, from upstream exploration and production to refining, the chemical industry and the sale of oil products. The other main function of the company was to give support to the local service, supply and contractor companies involved in offshore oil and gas activities.

The concerted efforts by the public and private sectors to run the management of their petroleum resources yielded remarkable results. In addition to optimal use of resources, the Norwegian model achieved two important positive outcomes: the advancement of offshore technology and an intergenerational income distribution scheme.

As mentioned earlier, the country was, at the beginning of the oil operations, completely dependent on other countries for the exploration and extraction of the resources from the sea, but it learned so quickly that it surprisingly surpassed the countries it depended on technologically in some areas. The determination to indigenise the operations of the gas and oil industry and the subsequent introduction of practical government guidelines in that endeavour, as well as the competent industrial base that the country possessed before the commencement of the oil operations, were the main contributing factors to that progress.

The technological advancement is perhaps the biggest achievement of the Norwegian model because that technology enabled effective production of petroleum resources, and it became instrumental in the drive for decarbonisation. Statoil is a world leader in the use of CCUS technology, whereby carbon dioxide is removed from gas and stored under the sea, and the same company is also leading the push toward renewables, notably wind energy. Norway made huge investments in wind energy and has big offshore wind energy projects both in Norway and in Europe, generating electricity from floating turbines.

As mentioned earlier, the petroleum service and supply industry pioneered offshore oil technology with the construction of rigs and platforms. The industry's exports generate a big part of the country's income, and it is the second-largest export industry after the sales of gas and oil. It is also a growing industry with great potential for further expansion.

The second biggest achievement is the distribution of income between present and future generations. Fair intergenerational distribution was an integral part of the plan and thus the debate was not about whether to share the resources with future generations, but merely how to put aside their portion. Specifically, the question was whether to designate some of the gas and oil fields for future generations and leave them untapped under the sea or whether to extract the resources and save the income from the sale of the resources for coming generations in the form of financial wealth.

The debate continued for some years because both proposals had valid points, and the advantages and disadvantages had to be weighed to reach a decision. The first argument was based on the assumption that because of technological advancements, it would be easier and cheaper to produce the resources in the future and for that reason, it would be best not to extract them. The other side argued that because of climate change and the consequent drive for the replacement of fossil fuels with renewables, oil and gas will lose their value and thus extracting them before that happens and keeping the income from the sale of these resources as financial wealth would be more beneficial to the coming generations. The second argument carried more weight, and eventually a decision was made in its favour.

The Norwegian Oil Fund, known today as the Government Pension Fund Global (GPF-G), was incepted in 1990 to administer the revenue from oil and gas put aside for future use. It is the world's largest sovereign fund, and since 1998 it has generated an annual return of over 6 percent. For the sake of risk diversification and value creation, the investments of the fund are spread worldwide. The fund has a stake in more than 9,000 companies spread over 73 countries and owns 1.4 percent of the shares of the world's listed companies, but most of the fund is invested in bonds, equity, real estate and infrastructure in renewable energies.

The fund manages financial wealth estimated at $1.4 trillion. The fund's intended goal is unique, its economic fundamentals are solid and it has already generated huge wealth that will be beneficial not only to future generations in Norway, but as a global investor primarily interested in renewables, it will also contribute to job creation and green energy worldwide.

The concerted effort by public and private sectors to develop and manage their resources on their terms, despite the initial lack of the necessary practical knowledge, paid off. The decision to develop strong local offshore industries capable of carrying out the required petroleum operations was implemented effectively. All in all, the Norwegian experiment has produced an exemplary resource management model, remarkable technological innovation and a pioneering intergenerational income distribution system. Indeed, it is an outstanding experiment that ought to be learned from.

5.2 Nigeria's Oil and Gas Industry Reform: Empowering the Nigerians

Oil exploration in Nigeria began in the first decade of the 20th century. A German company registered in the UK called the Nigerian Bitumen Corporation commenced the exploration activity in 1908 in Araromi and Okitipupa. It drilled 14 wells there, but it did not find any oil when its operations were halted by the First World War. In 1937, oil exploration operations resumed with another foreign company, Shell D'Arcy, which in 1956 changed its name to Shell-BP Petroleum Development Company of Nigeria Limited, after Shell D'Arcy and British Petroleum (BP) made a joint venture agreement. The joint venture was awarded the sole concessionary rights covering the whole territory of Nigeria, but the activities of Shell-BP were interrupted by the Second World War. Oil prospecting resumed after the Second World War in 1947, and commercial value oil was discovered in 1956 at Oloibiri in the Niger Delta region after half a century of exploration by Shell-BP, which was at the time the sole concessionaire.

Production from the Oloibiri field commenced in 1958 at an initial rate of 5,100 barrels per day, and shipment of oil also started in the same year, and that development paved the way for the expansion of oil exploration activities. Several oil companies were given concession rights in 1959, which included Mobil, Tenneco, Agip and Elf, and because of the expansion of the exploration activities, the production of oil grew quickly.

However, the Nigerian civil war (1967-70), also known as the Biafran War, negatively impacted the Nigerian oil industry. The home of the oil industry, the Niger Delta region, was the epicentre of the conflict and an independence declaration by separatists from the region triggered the war. The government declared war on the secessionists, and although the conflict was protracted, it eventually outmanoeuvred them. The rebel fighters surrendered in 1968, but there was no peace until 1970, when the conflict ended officially.

As a result of the termination of the civil war and a rise in global oil prices, which coincided with the signing of the peace deal, the industry was revitalised rapidly and production rose to 2 million barrels per day in early 1970s. Nigeria joined the Organisation of Petroleum Exporting Countries (OPEC) in 1971 and established the Nigerian National Petroleum Company (NNPC) in 1977, a state-owned company that was responsible for the administration of both the upstream and downstream sectors.

Nigeria is today Africa's largest oil- and gas-producing country, and it is the 11th largest producer of oil and gas in the world. Its production capacity is well over 3 million barrels per day, but due to OPEC's quota system and price shocks, its actual production rate has fluctuated and was on average below its capacity level: it has been producing on average about 2 million barrels a day since the early 1970s, although it is experiencing for the time being an all-time low level of production, which is lower than the average level. Oil and gas revenue accounts for over 90 percent of the country's export earnings, over 80 percent of the state revenue and nearly 10 percent of the GDP. The proven reserves of oil and gas are estimated at about 37,046 billion barrels and 208.62 trillion cubic feet, respectively.

Despite the huge petroleum reserves and the heavy income yield of oil, the industry has not lived up to its potential, to say the least, due to the lack of sovereign rights, mismanagement and unjust distribution of oil and gas revenues. Firstly, the Nigerian people, especially the local people at oil production locations, bore the brunt of the environmental devastation caused by the oil and gas industry, while the oil companies got the lion's share of the benefits. Secondly, the oil industry impacted the development of the other sectors of the economy negatively instead of improving them, and in particular pushed the agriculture industry, which yields the biggest contribution to the GDP, into the background.

In a sharp contrast to the Norwegian situation, where the oil operation began with the demarcation of its continental shelf, the declaration of sovereign ownership of the resources in the shelf and the management of the resources by the national authorities, Nigeria's oil industry started as an enterprise owned and led by foreigners. That lack of sovereign ownership over the resources and the management of the industry by foreign companies adversely impacted the development of the industry from the outset.

The colonial authorities started the oil exploration in Nigeria and the country was still under colonial rule when oil was discovered. Since the Nigerian people were not in charge of their country, they were not in a position to provide regulations for the management of their natural resources. The country gained its independence in October 1960, and until 1969, when the new independent nation enacted the Petroleum Act, the regulations enacted by the colonial authorities were used for the management of the industry.

Colonial oil exploration further established two additional trends that would characterise the Nigerian oil industry in the independence era: firstly, that oil was a national priority for the country regardless of its environmental and social adverse impacts, and second, that the oil industry, from the outset, formed an enclave in the broader Nigerian economy with limited interaction with the general Nigerian economy beyond the utilisation of local labour.

Despite the attainment of independence, the introduction of the Petroleum Act in 1969 and the establishment of the NNPC in 1977, the Nigerian oil industry remains an entity whose management is heavily influenced by foreigners and with little interaction with the country's broader economy. The participation of the indigenous business community in the industry is limited and, apart from the utilisation of local labour, the Nigerian people have little involvement in petroleum operations.

Due to the technological gap, the limited interaction between the emerging oil industry and the general economy and a lack of political direction to take over the running of oil and gas operations, the indigenisation of the industry was not a priority issue before the introduction of the Petroleum Industry Act (PIA). The government's main concern was revenue, and the country did not possess the technology to produce oil, and thus the authorities relied on foreign companies to do the practical work. In other words, the government neither developed strategies to acquire the required technologies for the exploration, extraction and development of oil and gas nor encouraged the locals to take part in the industry prior to the reform.

Although, like the colonial authority, the Nigerian government gave national priority to the oil and gas industry and the country's economic development strategy was preoccupied with that industry, the country did not develop a comprehensive management model for the oil and gas industry. Consequently, the country did not only remain dependent on foreigners for the utilisation of its fossil fuels, but the oil wealth did not reach the local inhabitants, despite the long period that the country has been producing oil. Besides that, the government undervalued the importance of the other sectors and divested itself of them. The sectors run by local people, such as agriculture, which the country used to depend on before the discovery of oil, were neglected, and as a result, underperformed. Additionally, the environmental impacts of the oil and gas activities and the marginalisation of the locals adversely affected the livelihoods of the communities living in the extraction areas, an effect that made their current living conditions worse than before the extraction of oil and gas began.

The prioritisation of the petroleum industry, its isolation from the other sectors of the broader economy, the lack of comprehensive development model, the displacement of the agricultural sector and the neglect of the environment had ramifications for the broader economy and the oil and gas industry. The agricultural sector accounts for about 24 percent of the country's GDP, and its contribution to GDP is 2.5 times larger than that of the petroleum sector. Nigeria has huge arable land and produces in huge quantities various agricultural products, which include palm oil, cocoa beans and sorghum. However, due to the prioritisation of oil and gas and the lack of a comprehensive development strategy, the country has not made use of the comparative advantage it possesses in the agricultural sector.

The strong pursuit for oil revenue by the NNPC and its foreign partners and their disregard for its negative impacts became one of the characteristics of the Nigerian oil and gas industry and the main cause of the problems of the industry today. The preoccupation with oil revenue and the lack of strategies regarding local capacity building and the indigenisation of the industry led to the subsequent economic marginalisation of the locals, which, in combination with the environmental problems caused by the industry, led to local discontent, which in turn adversely affected the industry.

The chase for petroleum revenue at the expense of human rights, the environment and the livelihoods of the population living in the extraction areas led to a conflict between the industry and the locals. Lack of local business participation in the oil and gas activities and the oil companies' determination to maximise the oil and gas wealth has led to a situation whereby the host communities get the full impacts of the environmental damage caused by the oil and gas operations without receiving any economic compensation. The impacts of the environmental damage include drinking water contamination, the destruction of agricultural land and forests caused by oil spills, gas flaring and climate change. Health and social problems that resulted from combination of these impacts and human rights abuses also affected the host communities.

In addition to these environmental, health and social problems, the government forcibly took land from the locals in the oil production areas, and it also imposed on them harsh punishments, which included long-term imprisonment and killing, when they protested. Nine protesters, including a prominent TV producer and writer, Ken Saro-Wiwa, were publicly hanged by the government in 1995. The human rights abuses and the adverse environmental impacts led to local resentment for the industry. They initially expressed their discontent via protests, but due to the frustration resulting from the harsh response from the authorities, the dissatisfaction of the local people towards the industry was afterwards expressed in the form of vandalism and sabotage.

Two decades ago, Nigeria recognised that the state of the oil and gas industry was inefficient at in-service deliveries and ineffective at promoting society's welfare objectives, and the discussion on how to correct the shortcomings took centre stage when the Oil and Gas Sector Reform Implementation Committee (OGIC) was inaugurated on April 24, 2000. The OGIC was instituted to review the situation of the industry and investigate how Nigeria could produce its recoverable energy reserves optimally. In other words, it had to find an answer to how the society's economic welfare could be maximised over time using the wealth derived from the produced and remaining oil and gas reserves in Nigeria. Specifically, the committee had to investigate the root causes of the failures and come up with recommendations to overcome them, and in addition to that, equity issues with respect to intergenerational wealth sharing, as well as wealth distribution among all current stakeholders (government, communities and operators) were to be examined by the committee.

The committee identified institutional and management failures and, in 2008, came up with recommendations requiring the restructuring of the industry. It demanded, amongst other things, the separation of commercial institutions from the regulatory and policy-making institutions and proposed the development of a petroleum policy framework requiring, amongst other things, the creation of a more efficient and commercially viable company, the protection of the environment and the initiation of the indigenisation of the industry with the encouragement of local businesses' participation in oil and gas operations and the empowerment of the host communities.

However, due to the complexity of the restructuring needed, disagreements over its terms between the government and the major oil companies operating in the country and changes of governments, the regulatory reform bill known as the PIA, the first version of which was submitted to the National Assembly in 2008, was delayed and was not finalised until August 2021. The reform bill was debated and rewritten several times, mainly because of disagreement between the oil companies and the state, and also between the executive and previous assemblies. The final version passed by parliament in 2021 approved the recommendations of OGIC, that is, the separation of the commercial institutions from the regulatory and policy-making institutions and the incorporation of a new petroleum company with limited liabilities, namely NNPC Limited. The adoption of an energy transition framework emphasising decarbonisation and environmental protection was also included in the reform document. Additionally, the PIA gives overriding priority to the participation of Nigerian businesses in the activities of the oil and gas industry and sees their input as key to the success of the reform package.

Under the PIA, new regulatory authorities were established: the Nigerian Upstream Petroleum Regulatory Commission, also known as 'the Commission', and the Nigerian Midstream and Downstream Petroleum Regulatory Authority, aka 'the Authority', replaced the Ministry of Petroleum in regulating the industry. The two new institutions are responsible for the technical and commercial regulations of oil and gas operations in their respective sectors and oversee the implementation of government policies regarding oil and gas operations, ensuring, amongst other things, strict implementation of environmental laws.

The transition of the NNPC into a limited company and the subsequent transfer of assets from the old NNPC to the new NNPC Limited were intended mainly to stimulate investment in the oil and gas sector. The setting up of a limited corporation, which conducts its affairs on a commercial basis, was the demand of the international oil companies and is meant to attract both foreign and local investors. Although NNPC Limited will continue to be government-owned, it is required to maintain the standards expected from a privately owned commercial entity, and such standards will lead to transparency and will make it easier for investors to do business with it.

The PIA deals with several domains, which include fiscal regime, funding and decarbonisation and energy transition. However, the core element of the reform package is the indigenisation of the industry by increasing the participation of the local business in the operations of the gas and oil industry to gain control of the management of the fossil fuel energy resources and make the industry an engine for the development of the whole economy.

The input of local businesses is especially crucial for the improvement of the delivery of services, for the increase in the efficiency of the industry and for the integration of the oil sector with the other segments of the economy. The indigenous businesses aim to realise these goals through, amongst other things, the expansion of local capacity and infrastructure development. Human capacity can be expanded through the advancement of entrepreneurship, technical progress and managerial skills. The development of the infrastructure will enhance the provision of local supply and services to the industry.

The aim of the indigenisation is to gain control of the management of the energy resources, stimulate economic growth and ensure the equitable distribution of oil and gas wealth. On the one hand, the industry must be indigenised as much as possible so that the Nigerians get a fair share of their wealth, and on the other hand, the country must not allow the current generation to use the entire gas and oil wealth derived from current energy production for their benefit. In other words, energy resources produced today must be used to develop durable infrastructure and human capital that will benefit and advance society for generations to come, and at the same time set aside a share of the derived wealth from oil and gas resources for the benefit of future generations.

With its new emphasis on indigenisation, the government changed its approach regarding the industry and introduced policy instruments intended to gain control of the operations and make the industry an engine for the development of the whole economy. To stimulate the growth of the indigenous capacity and to indigenise the industry as much as possible, the authorities promoted a framework that guarantees the active participation of Nigerians in oil and gas activities without compromising standards. Local business participation in all levels of oil operations (upstream, midstream and downstream) are now requirements, and foreign oil companies should present the activities set aside for the local business in their bid. Specifically, all fixed platforms (offshore and onshore), piles, anchors, buoys, bridges, flare booms and storage tanks are to be fabricated in Nigeria to maximise the utilisation of local fabrication yards.

In other words, Nigerian raw materials and locally manufactured goods and equipment are to be utilised, and the local people must be the main providers of labour and downstream services. In short, the jobs and services that can be done by Nigerians are to be taken by Nigerians, and all the sectors of the economy are now encouraged to take part in the operations of the oil and gas industry so that all the segments of the economy get a share of the benefits from the oil and gas sector.

To further empower local businesses, the Nigerian authorities introduced several capacity-building measures aimed at enhancing the local suppliers. These measures include project financing and funding of local businesses, identifying new opportunities for local suppliers, training Nigerians in targeted areas of competency, the acquisition of technological and managerial capability, the development of infrastructure and upgrading facilities.

Other obligations of the PIA include the protection of the environment and improving the living conditions of the host community. In compliance with the international decarbonisation drive, which aims to reduce emissions in the short term and eliminate them in the long term to protect the environment, Nigeria made a commitment at the COP26 meetings in Glasgow, UK, to reach net zero by 2060. However, Nigeria must deal first with its pressing domestic environmental problems affecting the livelihoods and living conditions of the host communities, as well as the security and stability of the country, before fulfilling global environmental pledges.

Pollution, deforestation, coastal erosion caused by carbon release into the atmosphere by diesel- and petrol-powered engines, gas flaring, exploration and extraction operations, sea bedrock removal and oil spills are the main domestic environmental problems related to the Nigerian gas and oil energy industry. In addition to the aforementioned regulatory reforms, the government aims to deal with these issues by restructuring the gas and petroleum liquid operations and by improving the relationship between the host communities and oil companies through the creation of an energy wealth redistribution mechanism.

The gas industry is important for both the implementation of the newly adapted environmental protection commitments and for the development of the economy, and therefore the restructuring of the gas sector is crucial both for optimisation and decarbonisation. The government aims to reach zero emissions by 2060 and has undertaken several measures to achieve that goal. Specific policies designed to promote the development and commercialisation of natural gas for domestic use and to further reduce carbon emissions were introduced. Gas is cleaner than oil and coal and therefore a preferable energy source. In addition to that, the country adopted an energy transition framework, of which gas is a major component. Gas does not only play a vital role in the energy transition framework but is cleanable energy that could be used in combination with renewables after the attainment of full decarbonisation or an acceptable level of emissions. Since gas is an energy transition resource, the reform of the gas industry is crucial to the decarbonisation drive. Furthermore, the government's decision to promote the development and commercialisation of natural gas for domestic use necessitates the implementation of gas-specific reform policies.

The National Gas Policy of 2017 and the regulations that followed, of which the PIA was the last, led to the restructuring of the administration of the gas industry. The government decided to move Nigeria from an oil-based economy to an oil- and gas-based industrial economy. Under the PIA, the Nigerian Gas Processing and Transportation Company (NGPTC) and the Nigerian Gas Marketing Company (NGMC) were established. In accordance with PIA guidelines, the authorities made commitments to eliminate gas flaring in the long term and reduce its social and environmental impacts in the short and medium terms. Additionally, the government adopted a National Gas Expansion Programme and decided to make gas the main power source of the country. Specifically, the authorities decided to use compressed natural gas (CNG) as the fuel for transportation, and LPG as the fuel for domestic cooking, captive power and small industrial complexes. To meet its domestic consumption demand for LPG, Nigeria will have to build gas treatment facilities that can produce the required gas products. The government also made a commitment to convert one million vehicles from diesel to gas power.

The PIA also provides structural changes to petroleum operations. The PIA requires that Nigeria constructs refineries for crude oil, storage facilities and transportation pipelines for its petroleum liquids.

The establishment of the host communities was prompted by the need to deal with conflict between the oil companies and locals caused by the economic marginalisation of the latter, local displacement related to the petroleum operations and the environmental degradation caused mainly by oil spills and gas flaring. The aim of the PIA with respect to host community affairs is to improve the relationship between the host communities and the oil companies by providing economic and social benefits from oil and gas operations through a development framework.

To implement these policies, the PIA obliges every oil company operating in the oil and gas producing region to incorporate a trust for the benefit of the host communities, which in turn will establish a fund, into which an amount equal to 3 percent of the oil company's actual annual operating expenditure of the preceding financial year shall be set aside for the applicable host community, and the trust committee must include one host community member. The oil companies are further required to carry out need assessments and develop them into a community development plan that identifies the projects to be undertaken by the trust. 75 percent of the trust funds should be earmarked for funding capital projects, 20 percent for funding a reserve fund and 5 percent for funding administrative running costs.

Although the 3 percent contribution is below the 10 percent the host communities demanded and they are not happy with the law provision imposing duties and responsibilities on each host community to protect oil and gas assets in its domain, the formation of the host communities and the subsequent interactions between the oil companies and the locals yielded positive results. The increasing cooperation between the host communities and oil companies reduced oil spills and vandalism. The economic marginalisation of the host communities, the environmental degradation that resulted from oil activities and the consequent conflict between the oil companies and the local people in the oil-producing region are not resolved, but the relationship between the two parties have improved and, consequently, oil spills and vandalism have been reduced. The resolution of the conflict between the host communities and the oil companies depends on the success of the whole reform package, which, as summarised below, is facing strong challenges.

Nigeria recognised that its dependency on international oil companies for the utilisation of its energy resources was its main obstacle in the way of the optimal use of these natural recourses. For this reason, the government sees the indigenisation of the industry as the solution to the problem. The reform package emphasises the importance of the participation of the local business in the operations of the industry and the economic support for the host communities. However, the full takeover of the operations of the oil activities is not easy and will certainly take time to realise, even though that goal is achievable.

The main bottlenecks in the indigenisation of the industry are corruption, divestment, the technological gap and political instability. As a result of these bottlenecks, the government is struggling to put the reform package into practice.

Corruption has been rampant in the government since the flow of oil money into the country began, and corrupt government officials and the multinational oil companies have been siphoning off much of the money generated from oil and gas sales. Mainly because of the corruption, the huge wealth flowing into the country from oil and gas revenues neither led to significant economic growth nor improved the living conditions of the population, as indicated by studies undertaken by independent bodies.

Due to the decarbonisation drive, vandalism and sabotage, oil and gas production became more costly. To fulfil the decarbonisation commitments undertaken by the government, the oil companies are required to reduce their carbon footprint, and this requirement increases the cost of oil production. Vandalism and sabotage are also external costs that increase the cost of oil operations. The combined effects of these externalities are divestment. International oil companies are discouraged from investing, especially in onshore activities, because of these external costs. They are largely disengaged from onshore exploration and production activities because of these external costs. Instead they concentrate on deep offshore operations, mainly because of tax exemptions on deep offshore activities.

In addition to rampant corruption and divestment pressure, there is a technological gap. Nigeria does not have the technological capacity which can enable it to step in and take over all the oil and gas operations, in the areas vacated by international oil companies and this constraint is an impediment to full utilisation of energy resources as well as the implementation of the planned projects like the construction of refineries, gas treatment facilities and fuel swap plans.

Other challenges of the PIA are security and related issues. Due to the activities of the terror group Boko Haram, which has paralysed the security of parts of the country, the economic marginalisation of the locals in the oil-producing areas and interstate quarrels, the Nigerian state is not functioning well. Insurgency, human rights abuses and the lack of coordination and coherence among the national institutions are adversely affecting the implementation of the PIA.

Despite these difficulties, Nigeria sees no alternative to the indigenisation of the industry and is determined to implement the reform package to the letter, and to that end took several steps. Through the joint projects in the upstream and midstream sectors, the country expects to achieve the technological transfer it needs to gain control of the oil and gas operations in the long term, though the divestment trend negatively impacts the technology transfer efforts. The domestic oil companies have taken over much of the onshore operations, and in the downstream sector, Nigerian businesses are running most of the retail and end-user services. On the supply side, local businesses are providing materials, and local subcontractors carry out many services for the petroleum industry, which includes pipeline services.

With these incremental steps, Nigeria aims to increase its capacity and attain full ownership of the operations of the industry. It sees the indigenisation of the industry and the empowerment of the people as the key to the attainment of the goal of optimal use of its energy resources, and the PIA outlines the strategy to achieve that. However, whether Nigeria succeeds in the indigenisation of the industry to utilise its oil and gas resources optimally, aside from external factors, depends on whether it succeeds in implementing the reform package.

The new Nigerian approach to the oil and gas industry in a way resembles the Norwegian one. In both cases, sovereign ownership of the resources and indigenisation of the operations of the oil and gas industry are the pillars of their oil and gas policy frameworks. The reformers of the Nigerian oil and gas industry seem to have learned from the Norwegian experience, and the PIA reform package was partly inspired by the successful Norwegian model.

6

Epilogue

6.1 The Scramble in Retrospect

The scramble for the Somali Region's natural energy resources began over a century ago. However, due to the illicit way the exploration of the resources commenced, neither did the scramble alliance achieve its economic objectives nor did the exploitation project bring any benefits to the region. On the contrary, the scramble proved to be a nightmare for the oil companies involved and caused human rights abuses, economic disaster and environmental and health damage for the inhabitants of the region.

The attempt of the Ethiopian government and its scramble associates to utilise the geological resources of the Somali Region at the expense of its inhabitants triggered resistance from the owners of the resources, who could not accept the robbery of their resources by foreign agents. Rejecting both the scramble alliance's quest for the exploitation of their geological resources and the occupation of their land, they resisted by first protesting and afterwards taking up arms when their peaceful protests were met with suppression. The consequent conflict between the resistance and the scramble alliance disrupted the exploration, extraction and utilisation of the natural energy resources and had grave consequences for the region, specifically for human rights, the environment, health, the economy and extraction of the geological resources.

For the foreign oil companies, the Ogaden Basin project has been, so far, a waste of money. They invested in it, some of them heavily, expecting to gain a fortune, but nearly all of them abandoned the project for security reasons without getting a return on their investment, by either voluntarily leaving or after their contracts were terminated by the government for failing to complete their contractual obligations. Their partner in the scramble project, namely the Ethiopian state, also did not profit from the project because of the conflict it created.

However, the biggest loser in the conflict that resulted from the scramble and the occupation is the Somali Region. As detailed in chapter 2, the negative impacts of the conflict on human rights, on livelihoods and the general economy, on the environment and on the geological resources themselves have been enormous.

The scramble alliance opted to forcibly seize the natural energy resources of the region, and the policy instruments pursued by the successive Ethiopian regimes to achieve that goal were suppression and human rights abuses. Imprisonment, extrajudicial killings and rape were some of the punishments frequently reported by human rights groups. Additionally, persistent collective punishment, which included a trade embargo, crackdowns, displacement and massacres turned the region into an open prison.

The scramble project adversely affected the livelihoods of the inhabitants in the Ogaden Basin because of the displacement and consequent loss of farmland, homes, properties and pasture lands. The uprooting of the people in the Basin as a result of the destruction of villages and the setting up of large exclusion zones, the trade embargo, the destruction and confiscation of property and crops and the general crackdown devastated the economy.

The clearing of land associated with exploration damaged the environment by leading to deforestation, and thereby desertification, habitat loss and the disruption of the environmental balance. Since the Ogaden Basin is around 350,000 square kilometres in size and the exploration sites are spread all over the Basin, deforestation affected a large area. In addition to that, reports of mystery diseases related to the project and believed to be caused by chemical spills have been circulating in the international media since 2020.

The illicit exploitation and the consequent conflict delayed the utilisation of the oil and gas resources in the region. As a result of that delay and the environmental pressure to get rid of fossil fuels, the value of natural energy resources is decreasing, and they may never be utilised because of the global decarbonisation drive if the postponement continues in the long term.

Despite the introduction of a general new law regulating the share of revenue from natural resources, so far nothing has changed in practical terms. The inhabitants of the region are still excluded from all stages of the project and the overall pattern of the scramble remains the same.

6.2 The Remedy

The remedy involves two things, namely the restoration of ownership of the geological resources to the region and the establishment of a proper business management framework that could ensure the fulfilment of all the sustainability conditions. The former is a prerequisite for peace, which in turn is a precondition for an environment conducive to the conduct of business. The latter is necessary for the optimal utilisation of the geological resources.

The history of the scramble demonstrated the incompatibility of illicit resource exploitation with peace. In other words, the exploitation of the geological resources of the region without the consent of its inhabitants will not be acceptable to them and hence a confrontation is unavoidable. The persistent illicit pursuit of the resources by the scramble alliance and the consequent resistance led to protracted conflict, which in turn has hindered the utilisation of the resources.

Despite the use of all possible force by the scramble alliance to suppress the inhabitants of the region in order to seize the natural energy resources, it neither succeeded in eliminating the resistance nor extracting the resources. A peaceful approach, recognizing the role of the region regarding its geological resources, followed by full or at least partial restoration of ownership of the resources to the inhabitants of the region where the resources are found, are preconditions for peace, which in turn is a prerequisite for an environment that's conducive to business.

Lessons learned from both the Norwegian and Nigerian experiments show the importance of property rights to the development of the oil and gas industry. The sovereign ownership of the continental shelf, which contains the gas and oil fields, and the subsequent indigenisation of the oil and gas industry were the main success factors of the exemplary Norwegian model. Nigeria's lack of success was largely associated with its colonial history and the running of the industry by foreign companies.

After the conflict in the Somali Region is resolved, the feasibility and sustainability of the project must be assessed, firstly from a business point of view and secondly from it's social, economic, environmental and health point of view to ensure optimal use of the resources. The former is about the profitability of the project and the latter is about the usefulness of the project for the lives of current and future generations of the whole society. Optimal use of the resources can be achieved only when the cost-benefit analyses of both considerations indicate the sustainability of the project.

To test the profitability of the oil and gas project, the costs related to exploration, extraction, production and transportation of the recoverable oil and gas reserves, and their market prices, need to be examined. The project becomes feasible when the expected profit exceeds the costs.

To achieve optimal use of the resources, the project must be both feasible and sustainable. The oil and gas project needs to be given multidimensional examinations from both micro and macro perspectives before its approval. Specifically, it should be profitable, adaptable to environmental and external challenges, and must address the issue of equitable revenue distribution among the current stakeholders as well as between the current and future generations.

6.3 The Forum under the Tree

The discussion of the nomads continues in the forum under the tree by reflecting on the scramble's history and contemplation about the future. The foreigners' relentless pursuit of the geological resources of the region without the consent of its inhabitants and the ensuing resistance against the scramble has shaped that history. The inhabitants recognise the importance of their geological resources to the development of their region, and therefore continuously debate how to defend them from the looters and create conditions for the optimal utilisation of their resources. The core issues under discussion in the forum are how to terminate the scramble project and deal with the current environmental, social, health and economic impacts of the ongoing illegal resource exploitation.

Despite the continued illicit exploitation, the history of the scramble has showed that without the consent of the inhabitants, it is highly unlikely that anyone will be able to utilise the geological resources of the region. The stop-start nature of the scramble caused by the campaign against it has emboldened the resistance and encouraged the locals to further defend their land and resources from the invading looters.

During the long period of the scramble and the subsequent resistance to it, the locals have learned a great deal about the behaviour of foreign oil companies and the systems of government of the countries they originated from, an experience that has enabled them to classify these companies and put them into different categories to take appropriate resistance measures against their exploitation activities. From the inception of the scramble until the 1990s, the oil companies have come from either the Western or Eastern alliance, and because of the difference in their system of government, the reactions of the companies to the resistance were different. Irrespective of local opposition, the Eastern alliance oil companies carried out their work using the military power provided to them by their governments and the host country, whereas the Western oil companies to some extent reacted to the local resistance and cancelled some of their contracts as a result.

The majority of the many companies that took part in the scramble since the 1990s terminated their contracts when they realised the extent of the local opposition, with the exception of the Chinese companies. The Chinese government initiated some of the

Chinese companies' engagement in the Ogaden Basin and, because of the heavy involvement of the Chinese government in the project and the authoritarian system of government there, the Chinese companies, like the Soviet ones, have not been responsive to local demands.

Due to the Chinese disregard for local indigenous rights and its persistent campaign to loot their resources, a Chinese oil company site was raided by the resistance in 2007. Despite the attack, the Chinese companies continued their oil and gas exploration operations because of the Chinese government's arrogant attitude.

The nomads debating under the tree and discussing the future of their oil and gas resources a long time ago reached a conclusion about what to do with these resources: they want to extract these resources and use them optimally, or leave them untapped under the ground if their use cannot be optimised. However, they are sidelined by the scramble alliance and since they are not in the driving seat, they are unable to manage their resources and are therefore primarily concentrating on preventing others from looting them.

Despite the exclusion of locals from the project, their resistance campaign has had a strong impact on the progress of the project, and they are widening the scope of that campaign. As a result of the long resistance and the vast experience the locals have gained during that period, the debate has been expanded, moving beyond the general deliberation and the concrete action for the defence of the resources by adding a new element of categorizing the exploiters in terms of the damage they cause. In other words, companies and their countries are to be listed and ranked in accordance with the ratio of the damage they inflict on the economy, the environment, human rights and the well-being of the indigenous society.

The aim of the categorisation is to prioritise the campaign against the worst offenders and polluters in the scramble and respond appropriately to those companies. Each company involved in the scramble is portrayed in accordance with its behaviour and the level of damage it inflicts by the participants of the forum, and they even coined nicknames for some companies that describe their perceived image in the local communities. For example, Western oil companies are referred to as noisy multifaceted exploiters because of the multiple messages coming from the West through their organisations: the oil hunters, the human rights advocates, the aid and relief organisations etc. The Chinese oil companies are nicknamed by the locals as the silent earth sweepers because of their self-imposed isolation from the local community, the environmental devastation they leave behind and their indiscriminate wildlife hunting, which does not even spare poisonous reptiles.

Although their best choice is a situation free from foreign intervention in the management of their resources, they are not waiting to act until that ideal opportunity becomes a reality. Given the current occupation and the ongoing scramble, they must act accordingly, concentrating on what is achievable under these circumstances.

Until recently, the Chinese companies held the main contract, but the indigenous inhabitants have a negative perception of them. They are given the worst rank by the inhabitants of the region because of their disregard for the rights of the indigenous inhabitants and their lack of a response to the compensation demands for the livelihood, economic, human rights, environmental and health damage they have inflicted on the region. Thus, the removal or the prevention of the reinstatement of Chinese companies is their immediate priority.

Although the inhabitants of the region aim to take over the management of their resources, they are not in control of their land and are therefore contemplating what to do in the meantime given that situation. Compared with Chinese companies, they see Western companies as the lesser of the two evils. Because of the relatively open mindset in the West and the increasing awareness of global environmental issues there, the locals would prefer them to temporarily replace the Chinese companies.

With both the immediate campaign to replace the Chinese companies with Western ones and the ultimate goal of getting sovereign rights over their land and its resources, as well as the indigenous management of the natural energy resources, the debate continues under the tree. The nomads are designing short-term measures to limit the negative impacts of the scramble and contemplating how to end the global scramble for their geological resources and are hopeful of a victory over the invading looters.

Notes and Bibliography

Chapter 1

1. Ethiopia Starts Oil Production from Ogaden, Dinknesh Ethiopia, 8 February 2020, https://dinkneshethiopia.com/2020/02/08/ethiopia-starts-oil-production-from-ogaden-basin/.
2. VICTOR KIPROP, Ethiopia begins production tests at Ogaden oilfield, The East African, June 30 2018, https://www.theeastafrican.co.ke/tea/business/ethiopia-begins-production-tests-at-ogaden-oilfield-1397200.
3. Ruari Phillips, Ethiopia Starts Oil Production from Ogaden Basin, Busiweek. Com, 4th July 2018, https://www.busiweek.com/ethiopia-starts-oil-production-from-ogaden-basin/.
4. Kaleyesus Bekele, Africa Oil to pull out of oil exploration blocks in Ogaden, (El-Kuran 3 not commercial), The Reporter, 30 August 2014, https://sites.google.com/site/linkstogeologyofethiopia/Mineral/africa-oil-ogaden.
5. Petroleum, Oil, and Gas in Ethiopia, History of Exploration, https://allaboutethio.com/petroleum-in-ethiopia-oil-gas-exploration-extraction.html.
6. Calub Hilala Fields - Geology of Ethiopia, sites.google.com, June 28 2018, https://sites.google.com/site/linkstogeologyofethiopia/Mineral/calub-hilala-fields.
7. M M Abdi, A history of the Ogaden (Western Somali) Struggle for Self Determination, Part II (2007–2021), pages 83-96 and 86-1991.

Chapter 2

1. M M Abdi, A history of the Ogaden (Western Somali) Struggle for Self Determination, Part I (1300-2007), pages 23-209.
2. M M Abdi, A history of the Ogaden (Western Somali) Struggle

for Self Determination, Part II (2007–2021), pages 9-97.

3. Ali, Juweria and Tom Gardner. 'The mystery sickness bringing death and dismay to eastern Ethiopia'. Guardian, October 15, 2020. https://www.theguardian.com/global-development/2020/feb/20/ the-mysterysickness-bringing-death-and-dismay-to-eastern-ethiopia.

Chapter 3

1. Louise Woodroofe, "Buried in the Sands of the Ogaden", The United States, the Horn of Africa and the Demise of Détente, The Kent State University Press 2013, pages 6-18.

2. M M Abdi, A history of the Ogaden (Western Somali) Struggle for Self Determination, Part I (1300-2007), pages 54-114.

3. M M Abdi, A history of the Ogaden (Western Somali) Struggle for Self Determination, Part II (2007–2021), pages, 83-96.

4. Mordechai Chaziza, China Consolidates Its Commercial Foothold in Djibouti, The Diplomat, January 26, 2021, https://thediplomat.com/2021/01/china-consolidates-its-commercial-foothold-in-djibouti/.

5. Congressional Research Service, China's Engagement in Djibouti, September 4, 2019, https://sgp.fas.org/crs/row/IF11304.pdf.

6. Hunter Baldridge, CHINA IN DJIBOUTI: A FUTURE UNCERTAIN, Observatory on Contemporary Crisis (OCC), 2022, https://crisesobservatory.es/china-in-djibouti-a-future-uncertain/.

7. Arba Gorash, The Role of Sinclair Petroleum in Federating Eritrea with Ethiopia, Tesfanews September 4, 2013, https://tesfanews.net/the-role-of-sinclair-oil-in-the-eritrea-ethiopia-federation/.

Chapter 4

1. United Nations, What is the United Nations Framework

Convention on Climate Change?, United Nations Climate Change 2022, https://unfccc.int/process-and-meetings/the-convention/what-is-the-united-nations-framework-convention-on-climate-change.

2. United Nations, What is the Kyoto Protocol?, United Nations Climate Change 2022, https://unfccc.int/kyoto_protocol.

3. United Nations, The Paris Agreement, United Nations Climate Change 2022, https://unfccc.int/process-and-meetings/the-paris-agreement/the-paris-agreement.

4. Reuters, Explainer: From Paris to Glasgow: cutting through climate jargon, Reuters 27 October, https://www.reuters.com/business/cop/paris-glasgow-cutting-through-climate-jargon-2021-10-27/.

5. Renewable Energy Market Size, Share Analysis | Growth Forecast, Allied Market research, September 2021, https://www.alliedmarketresearch.com/renewable-energy-market.

6. Renewables – Global Energy Review 2021 – Analysis – IEA, Renewables – Global Energy Review 2021 – Analysis – IEA https://www.iea.org › reports › renewables.

7. Mordor intelligence, Solar Energy Market Size, Trend | Industry Analysis and …2019-2027, https://www.mordorintelligence.com/industry-reports/solar-energy-market.

8. Endless Energy, A Brief History of Solar Power: Timeline & Today, https://www.goendlessenergy.com/brief-history-solar-power/.

9. IRENA, Wind - International Renewable Energy Agency, https://www.irena.org/wind.

10. Kyra Buckley, What you need to know about carbon capture, and how companies plan to use it, Houston Chronicle, June 24, 2022, https://www.houstonchronicle.com/business/energy/article/What-you-need-to-know-about-carbon-capture-and-17263296.php.

Chapter 5

1. Norwegian Ministry of Petroleum and Energy, Norway's Petroleum History, Norwegianpetroleum.no, July 22, https://www.norskpetroleum.no/en/framework/norways-petroleum-history/.

2. Helge Ryggvik, A Short History of the Norwegian Oil Industry: From Protected National Champions to Internationally Competitive Multinationals, Cambridge University Press 2015, https://www.cambridge.org/core/services/aop-cambridge-core/content/view/S0007680515000045.

3. Regjeringen, Norway's oil history in 5 minutes – regjeringen.no 2021, https://www.regjeringen.no/en/topics/energy/oil-and-gas/norways-oil-history-in-5-minutes/id440538/.

4. Isochukwu, BRIEF HISTORY OF OIL AND GAS IN NIGERIA, isochukwu.com, July 2018, https://isochukwu.com/2018/07/09/brief-history-of-oil-and-gas-in-nigeria/.

5. Recent Reform of Nigeria's Oil and Gas Industry Key Considerations, www.ashurst.com, November 2021, https://www.ashurst.com/en/news-and-insights/legal-updates/recent-reform-of-nigerias-oil-and-gas-industry-key-considerations/.

6. Matthew Culver, Legislative reform benefits Nigerian oil investment, www.energyvoice.com, January 2022, https://www.energyvoice.com/opinion/377457/nigeria-pia-financing-options/.

7. Okechukwu Nnodim, Nigeria's oil reserves hit 37.046 billion barrels, gas, 208.62TCF–FG, punchng.com, 7 May 2022, https://punchng.com/nigerias-oil-reserves-hit-37-046-billion-barrels-gas-208-62tcf-fg/.

8. Aaron O'Neill, Nigeria: Distribution of gross domestic product (GDP) across economic sectors from 2010 to 2020, Statista.com, Feb 15 2022, https://www.statista.com/statistics/382311/nigeria-gdp-distribution-across-economic-sectors/.

Index

Adigala Basin, 17
Africa Oil, 14, 16, 135
AFRICOM, 75
Al-Itihad, 31, 39, 40, 41
Assab, 77

Calub, 9, 10, 12, 14, 15, 16, 18, 135
CCUS, 99, 102, 111
COP21, 92, 93
COP26, 92, 93, 121

Damerdjog, 19
Dervish, 30
Dohar, 18

East Exploration Limited, 16
El-Kuraan, 16

GAIL India Limited, 13
Gewerkschaft Elwerath, 9, 10
Geysh, 31
GPF-G, 112

Hilala, 9, 10, 14, 15, 16, 18, 19, 135

IRENA, 94, 95, 137

Kalub Gas Share Company, 12, 13
Ken Saro-Wiwa, 117

Kyoto Protocol, 92, 137

Lundin East Africa, 13

Methanol, 13, 15

Nasrullah, 31, 60, 62
NNPC, 113, 115, 116, 118, 119
NSAI, 18, 77

OAU, 61, 62
Obale, 15, 32, 42, 48, 76
OGIC, 117, 118
ONLF, 15, 31, 40, 41, 42, 43, 48
OPEC, 113, 114

Petro Trans Company Ltd, 11, 13
PIA, 115, 118, 119, 121, 122, 123, 125, 126
POLY-GCL, 11, 14, 17, 18, 19, 20, 21, 22, 56, 73, 74, 76, 77, 78
Prince Sadruddin Aga Khan, 38

SALT II, 69, 72
Sicor Inc., 13, 14
SIL, 13, 15
Sinclair Oil Corporation, 8, 9, 10
Southwest Energy (HK) Ltd, 13
SPEE, 9, 10, 73
Standard Oil Company, 7, 29

Statoil, 109, 110, 111

SYL, 31, 34

Tenneco Oil Exploration, 8, 9, 10

UNFCCC, 92

WSLF, 31, 62

Zbigniew Brzezinski, 71

ZPEB, 11, 14, 15